Stand By Me

Hebrew Prayers for All Believers

ISRAƐL365

Stand
By Me

*Hebrew Prayers
for All Believers*

VOLUME 1

Edited by Shira Schechter and Rabbi Tuly Weisz

Dedication

I T WAS BY divine decree that Harvey Paul Oshman (חיים בן אנשיל) of blessed memory was created for his purpose in this world and was born only ten days after Israel was reborn in the beautiful year of 1948.

Harvey's days were filled with life-giving service to others. As a clinical psychologist, he saved many people on the brink of despair. And as he would often say, "It was only through much prayer, Hashem's (God's) help and by teaching them principles of Torah."

I can think of no more appropriate book to dedicate in his memory than this book of prayers, *Stand By Me*, in honor of one who always fervently stood alongside so many others on their challenging journeys.

May the words of these psalms and prayers that have been recited, whispered, and extolled throughout the ages bring about what King David pleaded for and what Harvey Oshman dedicated his life to: Hashem's restoration of our souls. May it be so.

Dedicated with love,
Trina Oshman

INTRODUCTION

Rabbi Tuly Weisz

A S AN ORTHODOX Jew, my daily life revolves around my prayer schedule. My phone's alarm clock wakes me up twenty minutes before morning prayers at my local synagogue, giving me just enough time to get dressed and join at least nine other men for the morning services. Later in the day, no matter how busy things are at the Israel365 office, our staff always stops in the middle of the day for afternoon prayers and to refocus our attention towards our Father in Heaven. Finally, after putting the kids to sleep and before beginning my usual routine of nightly phone calls, I slip out of the house to pray the evening service.

Unlike Christian prayer, which is often spontaneous and personal, Jewish prayer follows a Hebrew liturgy established over two thousand years ago. Personally, it's a great source of comfort to know that when I am praying, I am reciting the same sacred words that my forefathers and foremothers used, going back many centuries.

But Jewish prayer goes back even further. The sages trace Judaism's three daily prayers back to the Patriarchs in the Book of Genesis. When the Bible says, "Abraham awoke in the morning to the place where he had stood before the Lord" (Genesis 19:27) it means that Abraham prayed in the morning, instructing us to do the same. Similarly, when it states, "Isaac went to meditate in the field toward evening" (Genesis 24:63), we interpret that to mean that Isaac taught us to pray in the afternoon. And finally, when "Jacob encountered the place and slept there" (Genesis 28:11), we extrapolate a third daily prayer, the evening service.

While there is something deeply grounding in the routine of our ancient texts, prayer is also exceedingly personal. We have a saying, that when we study the Bible, God speaks to us, but when we pray, we are speaking to God. Jewish prayers take into account that we all have different hopes and fears, challenges and dreams. Yet in many ways, our prayers bring us together. Who has not encountered times of great distress, the illness of a loved one or financial uncertainty and cried out to God with a broken heart? Similarly, life often brings great blessings, and even miracles, for which our sincere gratitude to the Almighty leads to an outpouring of praise and thanksgiving.

Over the generations, our sages and scholars have written beautiful Hebrew prayers for all of life's ups and downs. These brilliant devotions are often interspersed with subtle Biblical quotations and references that connect our contemporary reality with the lofty words of the Hebrew prophets, poets and kings. Until now, these precious Jewish prayers have been off limits and inaccessible to English speakers and non-Jews. We are therefore pleased to introduce **Stand By Me: Hebrew Prayers for All Believers**, for the first time bringing classic Hebrew prayers to a broader community of Jews and non-Jews who seek to connect with the God of Israel through the timeless prayers of the people of Israel.

There has never been a more important time to turn our collective hearts in prayer towards the God of Israel. Following the devastating attack of October 7th, 2023 and the global wave of antisemitism that ensued, Israel has been demonized and isolated like never before. It is thus my fervent prayer that *Stand By Me: Hebrew Prayers for All Believers* serves to bring faithful Jews and Christians closer to each other and to our Father in Heaven. May the God of Abraham, Isaac and Jacob restore Jerusalem so that our holy city becomes the site of the "House of prayer for all nations" (Isaiah 56:7) and fulfill His promise, "I will transform the nations with a pure language for them all to call in the name of the Lord, and serve Him in unity." (Zephaniah 3:9)

Rabbi Tuly Weisz
Beit Shemesh, Israel

Table of Contents

Psalms for Times of Trouble or Distress

T HE PEOPLE OF Israel have always turned to the Book of Psalms in moments of both happiness and hardship, whether personal or collective. In times of trouble, they find solace in King David's timeless prayers, seeking divine compassion and relief. And in times of joy, they celebrate with these ancient songs, giving thanks and expressing gratitude for their blessings and moments of triumph.

The Sages teach that when writing the Psalms, King David thought not only of himself and his circumstances but of all generations and every possible situation. Regardless of one's identity or predicament, the Psalms resonate with the deepest emotions of the human heart. The following Psalms are those most commonly recited in times of trouble and distress.

Psalm 20

P SALM 20 IS a heartfelt plea for God's help in our darkest hours. While we must invest our own efforts to overcome challenges, this psalm reminds us that our salvation ultimately comes from God. Those who rely only on their own strength will fail, but those who put their trust in God will find the courage to face any challenge.

For the leader. A psalm of David. May the Lord answer you in time of trouble, may the name of the God of Jacob keep you safe. May He send you help from the sanctuary, and sustain you from Zion. May He receive the tokens of all your meal offerings, and approve your burnt offerings. **Selah**. *May He grant you your desire, and fulfill your every plan. May we shout for joy in your victory, arrayed by standards in the name of our God. May the Lord fulfill your every wish. Now I know that the Lord will give victory to His anointed; He will answer him from His heavenly sanctuary with the mighty victories of His right arm. They call on chariots, they call on horses, but we call on the name of the Lord our God. They collapse and lie fallen, but we rally and gather strength. O Lord, grant victory! May the King answer us when we call.*

Lammenatzeach mizmor ledavid.	לַמְנַצֵּחַ מִזְמוֹר לְדָוִד:
Ya'ancha adonai beyom tzarah	יַעַנְךָ יְהֹוָה בְּיוֹם צָרָה
yesaggevcha sheim elohei	יְשַׂגֶּבְךָ שֵׁם אֱלֹהֵי
ya'akov. Yishlach-ezrecha	יַעֲקֹב: יִשְׁלַח־עֶזְרְךָ
mikkodesh umitziyyon yis'adekka.	מִקֹּדֶשׁ וּמִצִּיּוֹן יִסְעָדֶךָּ:
Yizkor kol-minchotecha	יִזְכֹּר כָּל־מִנְחֹתֶךָ
v'eolatecha yedasheneh selah.	וְעוֹלָתְךָ יְדַשְּׁנֶה סֶלָה:

Yitten-lecha chilvavecha vechol-atzatecha yemalle. Nerannenah bishu'atecha uvesheim-eloheinu nidgol yemallei adonai kol-mish'aloteicha. Attah yada'ti ki hoshia' adonai meshicho ya'aneihu mishemei kodsho bigvurot yeisha yemino. eilleh varechev ve'eilleh vassusim va'anachnu besheim-adonai eloheinu nazkir. heimmah kare'u venafalu va'anachnu kamnu vannit'odad. Adonai hoshi'ah hammelech ya'aneinu veyom-kor'einu:

יִתֶּן־לְךָ כִלְבָבֶךָ וְכָל־
עֲצָתְךָ יְמַלֵּא: נְרַנְּנָה
בִּישׁוּעָתֶךָ וּבְשֵׁם־אֱלֹהֵינוּ
נִדְגֹּל יְמַלֵּא יְהוָֹה כָּל־
מִשְׁאֲלוֹתֶיךָ: עַתָּה יָדַעְתִּי
כִּי הוֹשִׁיעַ יְהוָֹה מְשִׁיחוֹ
יַעֲנֵהוּ מִשְּׁמֵי קָדְשׁוֹ
בִּגְבֻרוֹת יֵשַׁע יְמִינוֹ: אֵלֶּה
בָרֶכֶב וְאֵלֶּה בַסּוּסִים
וַאֲנַחְנוּ בְּשֵׁם־יְהוָֹה
אֱלֹהֵינוּ נַזְכִּיר: הֵמָּה כָּרְעוּ
וְנָפָלוּ וַאֲנַחְנוּ קַּמְנוּ
וַנִּתְעוֹדָד: יְהוָֹה הוֹשִׁיעָה
הַמֶּלֶךְ יַעֲנֵנוּ בְיוֹם־
קָרְאֵנוּ:

Notes

_____

_____

_____

_____

_____

_____

_____

_____

_____

Psalm 121

PSALM 121 GIVES us hope during challenging times by declaring that the Lord is our guardian and protector. Unlike a human guard, "the guardian of Israel neither slumbers nor sleeps." God's watchful eye never strays from His children, offering constant vigilance day and night.

A song for ascents. I turn my eyes to the mountains; from where will my help come? My help comes from the Lord, maker of heaven and earth. He will not let your foot give way; your guardian will not slumber; See, the guardian of Israel neither slumbers nor sleeps! The Lord is your guardian, the Lord is your protection at your right hand. By day the sun will not strike you, nor the moon by night. The Lord will guard you from all harm; He will guard your life. The Lord will guard your going and coming now and forever.

Shir lamma'alot essa einai el-heharim mei'ayin yavo ezri. Ezri me'im adonai oseih shamayim va'aretz. Al-yitten lammot raglecha al-yanum shomerecha. Hinneh lo-yanum velo yishan shomer yisra'el. Adonai shomerecha adonai tzillecha al-yad yeminecha. Yomam hashemesh lo-yakkekkah veyarei'ach ballayelah. Adonai yishmorcha mikkol-ra yishmor et-nafshecha. Adonai yishmor-tzeitcha uvo'echa mei'attah ve'ad-olam.

שִׁיר לַמַּעֲלוֹת אֶשָּׂא עֵינַי אֶל־הֶהָרִים מֵאַיִן יָבֹא עֶזְרִי: עֶזְרִי מֵעִם יְהֹוָה עֹשֵׂה שָׁמַיִם וָאָרֶץ: אַל־יִתֵּן לַמּוֹט רַגְלֶךָ אַל־יָנוּם שֹׁמְרֶךָ: הִנֵּה לֹא־יָנוּם וְלֹא יִישָׁן שׁוֹמֵר יִשְׂרָאֵל: יְהֹוָה שֹׁמְרֶךָ יְהֹוָה צִלְּךָ עַל־יַד יְמִינֶךָ: יוֹמָם הַשֶּׁמֶשׁ לֹא־יַכֶּכָּה וְיָרֵחַ בַּלָּיְלָה: יְהֹוָה יִשְׁמָרְךָ מִכָּל־רָע יִשְׁמֹר אֶת־נַפְשֶׁךָ: יְהֹוָה יִשְׁמָר־צֵאתְךָ וּבוֹאֶךָ מֵעַתָּה וְעַד־עוֹלָם:

Psalm 130

IN PSALM 130 we cry out to God from the depths. This psalm is often understood as a cry from the depths of despair, but Rabbi Joseph B. Soloveitchik understood it on an even deeper level: this is a cry from the deepest recesses of our souls, the part of us that has not been affected by sin. From that deep place we call out to God for help, urging Him to see beyond our external faults to our true inner selves, and to grant us salvation. The psalm describes our anticipation for God as greater than a watchman's wait for dawn. Just as we trust the sun to rise every day, we are confident in God's promise of salvation and redemption.

A song of ascents. Out of the depths I call You, O Lord. O Lord, listen to my cry; let Your ears be attentive to my plea for mercy. If You keep account of sins, O Lord, Lord, who will survive? Yours is the power to forgive so that You may be held in awe. I look to the Lord; I look to Him; I await His word. I am more eager for the Lord than watchmen for the morning, watchmen for the morning. O Israel, wait for the Lord; for with the Lord is steadfast love and great power to redeem. It is He who will redeem Israel from all their iniquities.

Shir hamma'alot mimma'amakkim
keraticha adonai. Adonai shim'ah
vekoli tihyenah oznecha kashuvot
lekol tachanunai. Im-avonot
tishmor-yah adonai mi ya'amod.
Ki-immecha hasselichah lema'an

שִׁיר הַמַּעֲלוֹת מִמַּעֲמַקִּים
קְרָאתִיךָ יְהֹוָה: אֲדֹנָי שִׁמְעָה
בְקוֹלִי תִּהְיֶינָה אָזְנֶיךָ קַשֻּׁבוֹת
לְקוֹל תַּחֲנוּנָי: אִם־עֲוֹנוֹת
תִּשְׁמָר־יָהּ אֲדֹנָי מִי יַעֲמֹד:
כִּי־עִמְּךָ הַסְּלִיחָה לְמַעַן

tivvarei. Kivviti adonai kivvetah nafshi velidvaro hochaleti. Nafshi ladonai mishomerim labboker shomerim labboker. Yachel yisra'el el-adonai ki-im-adonai hachesed veharbeih immo fedut. Vehu yifdeh et-yisra'el mikkol avonotav.

תֵּרֶא: קִוִּיתִי יְהֹוָה קִוְּתָה נַפְשִׁי וְלִדְבָרוֹ הוֹחָלְתִּי: נַפְשִׁי לַאדֹנָי מִשֹּׁמְרִים לַבֹּקֶר שֹׁמְרִים לַבֹּקֶר: יַחֵל יִשְׂרָאֵל אֶל־יְהֹוָה כִּי־עִם־יְהֹוָה הַחֶסֶד וְהַרְבֵּה עִמּוֹ פְדוּת: וְהוּא יִפְדֶּה אֶת־יִשְׂרָאֵל מִכֹּל עֲוֹנֹתָיו:

Notes

_____

_____

_____

_____

_____

_____

_____

_____

_____

_____

_____

_____

_____

_____

_____

_____

_____

_____

Psalm 142

D AVID RECITES PSALM 142 after he is forced to run for his
life and find refuge in a cave in Adullam (I Samuel 22).
In the cold, dark cave, as he is being chased and pursued,
David lifts up his voice and pours out his heart to God.
Though he felt friendless and lonely, David was not alone.
God was there with him, listening, just as He is always lis-
tening to us.

*A maskil of David, while he was in the cave. A prayer. I cry aloud
to the Lord; I appeal to the Lord loudly for mercy. I pour out my
complaint before Him; I lay my trouble before Him when my spirit
fails within me. You know my course; they have laid a trap in the
path I walk. Look at my right and see—I have no friend; there is
nowhere I can flee, no one cares about me. So I cry to You, O Lord;
I say, "You are my refuge, all I have in the land of the living." Listen
to my cry, for I have been brought very low; save me from my
pursuers, for they are too strong for me. Free me from prison, that
I may praise Your name. The righteous shall glory in me for Your
gracious dealings with me.*

Maskil ledavid bihyoto
vamme'arah tefillah. Koli el-adonai
ez'ak koli el-adonai etchannan.
Eshpoch lefanav sichi tzarati
lefanav aggid. Behit'atteif alai
ruchi ve'attah yada'ta netivati
be'orach-zu ahalleich tamenu fach
li. Habbeit yamin ure'eh ve'ein-li

מַשְׂכִּיל לְדָוִד בִּהְיוֹתוֹ
בַמְּעָרָה תְפִלָּה: קוֹלִי אֶל־יְהֹוָה
אֶזְעָק קוֹלִי אֶל־יְהֹוָה אֶתְחַנָּן:
אֶשְׁפֹּךְ לְפָנָיו שִׂיחִי צָרָתִי
לְפָנָיו אַגִּיד: בְּהִתְעַטֵּף עָלַי
רוּחִי וְאַתָּה יָדַעְתָּ נְתִיבָתִי
בְּאֹרַח־זוּ אֲהַלֵּךְ טָמְנוּ פַח
לִי: הַבֵּיט יָמִין וּרְאֵה וְאֵין־לִי

makkir avad manos mimmenni ein
doresh lenafshi. Za'akti eleicha
adonai amarti attah machsi chelki
be'eretz hachayyim. Hakshivah
el-rinnati ki-dalloti me'od hatzileini
merodefai ki ametzu mimmenni.
Hotzi'ah mimmasger nafshi
lehodot et-shemecha bi yachtiru
tzaddikim ki tigmol alai.

מַכִּיר אָבַד מָנוֹס מִמֶּנִּי אֵין
דוֹרֵשׁ לְנַפְשִׁי: זָעַקְתִּי אֵלֶיךָ
יְהֹוָה אָמַרְתִּי אַתָּה מַחְסִי חֶלְקִי
בְּאֶרֶץ הַחַיִּים: הַקְשִׁיבָה
אֶל־רִנָּתִי כִּי־דַלּוֹתִי מְאֹד הַצִּילֵנִי
מֵרֹדְפַי כִּי אָמְצוּ מִמֶּנִּי:
הוֹצִיאָה מִמַּסְגֵּר נַפְשִׁי
לְהוֹדוֹת אֶת־שְׁמֶךָ בִּי יַכְתִּרוּ
צַדִּיקִים כִּי תִגְמֹל עָלָי:

Notes

_____

_____

_____

_____

_____

_____

_____

_____

_____

_____

_____

_____

_____

_____

Prayers for Healing

WHILE WE RELY heavily on modern medicine, the Bible teaches us that it is really God who is the source of all healing, as it says in Exodus 15:26, "I am the Lord your healer." In addition to seeking medical interventions, we must also turn to God when faced with illness. Ultimately, our health rests in His compassionate hands.

In addition to turning to God when we are sick, we must also pray for the health of others. When we do so, we are not only acknowledging God's supreme role as the ultimate healer, but we are fulfilling the command to "Love your neighbor as yourself," as well as performing an act of kindness for the one who is ill.

Prayer for the sick is actually a practice that is deeply rooted in Jewish tradition and finds precedent in the Bible. Moses himself uttered a simple yet powerful prayer for the recovery of his sister: "O God, pray heal her!" (Numbers 12:13). Our prayers can have a profound impact.

Prayer for Healing and Deliverance from the Daily Prayers

Heal us, Lord, and we will be healed, deliver us and we will be delivered; for You are our praise. Grant a complete healing to all our affliction because You are the Almighty, King, Who is a faithful and merciful Healer. Blessed are You, Lord, Healer of the sick of His people Israel.

Refa'einu adonai veneirafei
hoshi'einu venivvashei'ah ki
tehillatenu attah veha'aleh refu'ah
sheleimah lechol makkoteinu ki el
melech rofe ne'eman verachaman
attah: baruch attah adonai rofei
cholei ammo yisra'el:

רְפָאֵנוּ יְהֹוָה וְנֵרָפֵא
הוֹשִׁיעֵנוּ וְנִוָּשֵׁעָה כִּי
תְהִלָּתֵנוּ אָתָּה וְהַעֲלֵה רְפוּאָה
שְׁלֵמָה לְכָל מַכּוֹתֵינוּ כִּי אֵל
מֶלֶךְ רוֹפֵא נֶאֱמָן וְרַחֲמָן
אָתָּה: בָּרוּךְ אַתָּה יְהֹוָה רוֹפֵא
חוֹלֵי עַמּוֹ יִשְׂרָאֵל:

Notes

_____

_____

_____

_____

_____

_____

_____

Prayer for a Man Who is Sick

*May He Who blessed our fathers, Abraham, Isaac and Jacob, Moses and Aaron, David and Solomon, bless and heal (insert **the name of the sick person**, son of **the sick person's mother's name**). May the Holy One, blessed be He, be filled with mercy for him, to restore him to health and to cure him, to strengthen him and to invigorate him. And may He hasten to send him from heaven a complete recovery to his 248 bodily parts and 365 veins, among the other sick people of Israel, a healing of spirit and a healing of body; Now, speedily, and in a time soon to come, and let us say, Amen.*

Mi shebbeirach avoteinu avraham yitzchak veya'akov mosheh ve'aharon david ushelomoh hu yevarech virappei et (insert *the name of the sick person,* son of *the sick person's mother's name*), hakkadosh baruch hu yimmalle rachamim alav lehachalimo ulerappe'oto ulehachaziko ulehachayoto, veyishlach lo meherah refu'ah sheleimah min hashamayim lerama"ch eivarav ushesa gidav betoch she'ar cholei yisra'el, refu'at hanefesh urefu'at hagguf, hashta ba'agala uvizman kariv. Venomar amen:

מִי שֶׁבֵּרַךְ אֲבוֹתֵינוּ אַבְרָהָם
יִצְחָק וְיַעֲקֹב מֹשֶׁה
וְאַהֲרֹן דָּוִד וּשְׁלֹמֹה הוּא
יְבָרֵךְ וִירַפֵּא אֶת
(פלוני בן
פלונית),
הַקָּדוֹשׁ בָּרוּךְ הוּא יְמַלֵּא
רַחֲמִים עָלָיו לְהַחֲלִימוֹ
וּלְרַפֹּאתוֹ וּלְהַחֲזִיקוֹ
וּלְהַחֲיוֹתוֹ, וְיִשְׁלַח לוֹ
מְהֵרָה רְפוּאָה שְׁלֵמָה מִן
הַשָּׁמַיִם לְרַמַ"ח אֵבָרָיו
וּשְׁסָ"ה גִּידָיו בְּתוֹךְ שְׁאָר חוֹלֵי
יִשְׂרָאֵל, רְפוּאַת הַנֶּפֶשׁ וּרְפוּאַת
הַגּוּף, הַשְׁתָּא בַּעֲגָלָא וּבִזְמַן
קָרִיב. וְנֹאמַר אָמֵן:

Prayer for a Woman Who is Sick

*May the one who blessed our ancestors, Abraham, Isaac, and Jacob, Moses and Aaron, David and Solomon bless (**insert the name of the sick person,** daughter of **the sick person's mother's name**). May the Holy One, Blessed Be God, be filled with mercy for her, to heal her and to strengthen her and to enliven her, and quickly send her a complete healing from heaven to all her limbs and organs, among the other sick of Israel, a healing of the spirit and a healing of the body. Now, speedily, and in a time soon to come, and let us say, Amen.*

Mi shebbeirach avoteinu avraham yitzchak veya'akov mosheh ve'aharon david ushelomoh hu yevarech et hacholah (insert *the name of the sick person,* daughter of *the sick person's mother's name*). hakkadosh baruch hu yimalei rachamim aleha lehachalimah ulerappetah ulehachazikah ulehachayotah, veyishlach lah meheirah refu'ah sheleimah min hashamayim lechol eivareha ulechol gideha betoch she'ar cholei yishra'el, refu'at hannefesh urefu'at hagguf hashta ba'agala uvizman kariv. Venomar amen:

מִי שֶׁבֵּרַךְ אֲבוֹתֵינוּ אַבְרָהָם יִצְחָק וְיַעֲקֹב מֹשֶׁה וְאַהֲרֹן דָּוִד וּשְׁלֹמֹה הוּא יְבָרֵךְ אֶת הַחוֹלָה (פלונית בת פלונית), הַקָּדוֹשׁ בָּרוּךְ הוּא יְמַלֵּא רַחֲמִים עָלֶיהָ לְהַחֲלִימָהּ וּלְרַפְּאתָהּ וּלְהַחֲזִיקָהּ וּלְהַחֲיוֹתָהּ, וְיִשְׁלַח לָהּ מְהֵרָה רְפוּאָה שְׁלֵמָה מִן הַשָּׁמַיִם לְכָל אֵבָרֶיהָ וּלְכָל גִּידֶיהָ בְּתוֹךְ שְׁאָר חוֹלֵי יִשְׂרָאֵל, רְפוּאַת הַנֶּפֶשׁ וּרְפוּאַת הַגּוּף הַשְׁתָּא בַּעֲגָלָא וּבִזְמַן קָרִיב. וְנֹאמַר אָמֵן:

Psalm to Recite for Those Who are Sick

WHEN PRAYING FOR someone who is ill, it is customary to recite Psalm 30 in addition to the Psalms recited in all times of distress above. Psalm 30 is a fitting psalm to recite when praying for recovery. Written by David as he reflected on his journey from despair to gratitude, this chapter resonates deeply with those praying for healing, especially through verse 3 which states "O Lord, my God, I cried out to You, and You healed me." Even in our darkest hours we are not forsaken, and in an instant God can lift us from any affliction into a state of redemption and comfort.

A psalm of David. A song for the dedication of the House. I extol You, O Lord, for You have lifted me up, and not let my enemies rejoice over me. O Lord, my God, I cried out to You, and You healed me. O Lord, You brought me up from Sheol, preserved me from going down into the Pit. O you faithful of the Lord, sing to Him, and praise His holy name. For He is angry but a moment, and when He is pleased there is life. One may lie down weeping at nightfall; but at dawn there are shouts of joy. When I was untroubled, I thought, "I shall never be shaken," for You, O Lord, when You were pleased, made [me] firm as a mighty mountain. When You hid Your face, I was terrified. I called to You, O Lord; to my Lord I made appeal, "What is to be gained from my death, from my descent into the Pit? Can dust praise You? Can it declare Your faithfulness? Hear, O Lord, and have mercy on me; O Lord, be my help!" You turned my lament into dancing, you undid my sackcloth and girded me with joy, that [my] whole being might sing hymns to You endlessly; O Lord my God, I will praise You forever.

Mizmor shir-chanukkat habbayit ledavid. Aromimcha adonai ki dillitani velo-simmacha oyevai li. Adonai elohai shivva'ti eleicha vattirpa'eini. Adonai he'elita min-she'ol nafshi chiyyitani miyyordi-vor. Zammeru ladonai chasidav vehodu lezecher kodsho. Ki rega be'appo chayyim birtzono ba'erev yalin bechi velabboker rinnah. Va'ani amarti veshalvi bal-emmot le'olam. Adonai birtzon'cha he'emadtah leharri-oz histarta fanecha hayiti nivhal. Eilecha adonai ekra ve'el-adonai etchannan. Mah-betza bedami beridti el-shachat hayodecha afar hayaggid amittecha. Shema-adonai vechonneini adonai heyeih-ozer li. Hafachta mispedi lemachol li pittachta sakki vatte'azzereini simchah. Lema'an yezammercha chavod velo yiddom adonai elohai le'olam odekka.

מִזְמוֹר שִׁיר־חֲנֻכַּת הַבַּיִת לְדָוִד: אֲרוֹמִמְךָ יְהוָה כִּי דִלִּיתָנִי וְלֹא־שִׂמַּחְתָּ אֹיְבַי לִי: יְהוָה אֱלֹהָי שִׁוַּעְתִּי אֵלֶיךָ וַתִּרְפָּאֵנִי: יְהוָה הֶעֱלִיתָ מִן־שְׁאוֹל נַפְשִׁי חִיִּיתַנִי מִיָּרְדִי־בוֹר: זַמְּרוּ לַיהוָה חֲסִידָיו וְהוֹדוּ לְזֵכֶר קָדְשׁוֹ: כִּי רֶגַע בְּאַפּוֹ חַיִּים בִּרְצוֹנוֹ בָּעֶרֶב יָלִין בֶּכִי וְלַבֹּקֶר רִנָּה: וַאֲנִי אָמַרְתִּי בְשַׁלְוִי בַּל־אֶמּוֹט לְעוֹלָם: יְהוָה בִּרְצוֹנְךָ הֶעֱמַדְתָּה לְהַרְרִי־עֹז הִסְתַּרְתָּ פָנֶיךָ הָיִיתִי נִבְהָל: אֵלֶיךָ יְהוָה אֶקְרָא וְאֶל־אֲדֹנָי אֶתְחַנָּן: מַה־בֶּצַע בְּדָמִי בְּרִדְתִּי אֶל־שָׁחַת הֲיוֹדְךָ עָפָר הֲיַגִּיד אֲמִתֶּךָ: שְׁמַע־יְהוָה וְחָנֵּנִי יְהוָה הֱיֵה־עֹזֵר לִי: הָפַכְתָּ מִסְפְּדִי לְמָחוֹל לִי פִּתַּחְתָּ שַׂקִּי וַתְּאַזְּרֵנִי שִׂמְחָה: לְמַעַן יְזַמֶּרְךָ כָבוֹד וְלֹא יִדֹּם יְהוָה אֱלֹהַי לְעוֹלָם אוֹדֶךָ:

Notes

_____

_____

_____

Prayer for Health

RABBI HAIM YOSEF David Azulai (1724 – 1806), one of the great Jewish sages of the eighteenth century, wrote the following prayer for health. It is an appeal to the Master of the Universe for strength, health, and resilience.

Master of the Universe, in Your mercy, grant us strength, health, and sufficient capability. Strengthen and fortify our limbs, sinews, and bodies to stand guard. Let no ailment or pain befall us, and let us be joyful, good, and healthy in Your service. Deliver us from all evil, lengthen our days in goodness and our years in pleasantness. Fill our years with long life, and add years of life to us for Your service. Under the shadow of Your wings, hide us and save us, us and all the members of our household, from all harsh and evil decrees. May we be calm and serene, flourishing and vibrant in Your service and in awe of You.

Ribbono shel olam,	רִבּוֹנוֹ שֶׁל עוֹלָם,
berachamecha tein banu koach	בְּרַחֲמֶיךָ תֵּן בָּנוּ כֹּחַ
uvri'ut v'yicholet maspik, vachazak	וּבְרִיאוּת וִיכֹלֶת מַסְפִּיק, וַחֲזַק
ve'ematz ba'avareinu vegideinu	וְאַמֵּץ בַּאֲבָרֵינוּ וְגִידֵינוּ
vegufeinu la'amod al hammishmar.	וְגוּפֵנוּ לַעֲמֹד עַל הַמִּשְׁמָר.
Velo ye'era lanu shum machosh	וְלֹא יֶאֱרַע לָנוּ שׁוּם מָחוֹשׁ
veshum ke'eiv, venihyeh	וְשׁוּם כְּאֵב, וְנִהְיֶה
semeichim vetovim uveri'im	שְׂמֵחִים וְטוֹבִים וּבְרִיאִים
la'avodatecha. Vetatzileinu	לַעֲבוֹדָתֶךָ. וְתַצִּילֵנוּ
mikkol ra, veta'arich yameinu	מִכָּל רַע, וְתַאֲרִיךְ יָמֵינוּ
betov ushenoteinu bin'imim	בְּטוֹב וּשְׁנוֹתֵינוּ בַּנְּעִימִים
umalei shenoteinu orech	וּמָלֵא שְׁנוֹתֵינוּ אֹרֶךְ

yamim, ushenot chayyim tosif lanu
la'avodatecha. Uv'tzeil kenafecha
tastireinnu, vetatzileinnu lanu
ulechol benei beitenu mikkol
gezerot kashot vera'ot, venihyeh
shekeitim vesha'anannim,
deshainim vera'anannim
la'avodatecha uleyir'atecha.

יָמִים, וּשְׁנוֹת חַיִּים תּוֹסִיף לָנוּ
לַעֲבוֹדָתֶךָ. וּבְצֵל כְּנָפֶיךָ
תַּסְתִּירֵנוּ, וְתַצִּילֵנוּ לָנוּ
וּלְכָל בְּנֵי בֵּיתֵנוּ מִכָּל
גְּזֵרוֹת קָשׁוֹת וְרָעוֹת, וְנִהְיֶה
שְׁקֵטִים וְשַׁאֲנַנִּים,
דְּשֵׁנִים וְרַעֲנַנִּים
לַעֲבוֹדָתֶךָ וּלְיִרְאָתֶךָ.

Notes

Prayer for Longevity

Rabbi Haim Yosef David Azulai (1724 – 1806), authored the following prayer for long life. The prayer seeks God's benevolence to cancel harsh decrees and provide sanctuary from various forms of suffering – including illness, fear, oppression, and mental confusion – that could hinder a long and healthy life.

"She is a tree of life to those who grasp her, and whoever holds on to her is happy. Her ways are pleasant ways, and all her paths, peaceful. The name of the Lord is a tower of strength To which the righteous man runs and is safe."

May it be Your will before You, Lord our God and God of our ancestors, that You fill us with mercy and act for the sake of our holy forefathers, Abraham who embodied kindness, Isaac who was adorned in strength, and Jacob who represented glory. Cancel from upon us all harsh and evil decrees, and hide us in the shadow of Your wings. Let us be healthy in all our limbs and sinews. Protect us from all trouble, all fear, and all illness. Save us from all kinds of oppression and confusion of mind. Let our hearts not be troubled, nor our eyes dimmed. Let us be settled in our minds, and grant us strength and health to serve and fear You.

Lengthen our days in goodness and pleasantness. In all that we turn to, let us understand, and in all that we do, let us succeed. Amen, may it be Your will. May Your kindness, Lord, be upon us, just as we have hoped in You. Show us, Lord, Your kindness, and give us Your salvation. I have trusted in Your kindness; my heart will rejoice in Your salvation. I will sing to the Lord, for He has been bountiful to me. Behold, God is my salvation; I will trust and not be afraid, for the Lord is my strength and might; He has become my deliverance.

"Eitz chayyim hi lemachazikim bah vetomecheha me'ushar. Deracheha darchei no'am vechol netivoteha shalom. Migdal oz sheim adonai bo yarutz tzaddik venisgav."

"עֵץ חַיִּים הִיא לְמַחֲזִיקִים בָּהּ וְתֹמְכֶיהָ מְאֻשָּׁר. דְּרָכֶיהָ דַרְכֵי נֹעַם וְכָל נְתִיבוֹתֶיהָ שָׁלוֹם. מִגְדַּל־עֹז שֵׁם יְהֹוָה בּוֹ־יָרוּץ צַדִּיק וְנִשְׂגָּב"

Yehi ratzon millefanecha adonai eloheinu ve'elohei avoteinu shettitmalle rachamim aleinu va'aseih lema'an avoteinu hakkedoshim, avraham ish hachesed, yitzchak ne'zar bigvurah, ya'akov kelil tif'eret. Utevatteil me'aleinu kol gezeirot kashot vera'ot, uvtzeil kenafecha tastireinu, venihyeh beri'im bechol eivareinu vegidenu, vetishmereinu mikkol tzarah umikkol pachad umikkol choli, vetatzileinu mikkol minei kishuf umibbilbul hada'at, ve'al yidveh libbeinu ve'al yechshechu eineinu. Venihyeh meyushavim beda'teinu, vetein banu koach uveri'ut la'avodatecha veyir'atecha.

יְהִי רָצוֹן מִלְּפָנֶיךָ יְיָ אֱלֹהֵינוּ וֵאלֹהֵי אֲבוֹתֵינוּ שֶׁתִּתְמַלֵּא רַחֲמִים עָלֵינוּ וַעֲשֵׂה לְמַעַן אֲבוֹתֵינוּ הַקְּדוֹשִׁים, אַבְרָהָם אִישׁ הַחֶסֶד, יִצְחָק נֶאֱזָר בִּגְבוּרָה, יַעֲקֹב כְּלִיל תִּפְאָרֶת. וּתְבַטֵּל מֵעָלֵינוּ כָּל גְּזֵרוֹת קָשׁוֹת וְרָעוֹת, וּבְצֵל כְּנָפֶיךָ תַּסְתִּירֵנוּ, וְנִהְיֶה בְּרִיאִים בְּכָל אֲבָרֵינוּ וְגִידֵנוּ, וְתִשְׁמְרֵנוּ מִכָּל צָרָה וּמִכָּל פַּחַד וּמִכָּל חֳלִי, וְתַצִּילֵנוּ מִכָּל מִינֵי כִּשּׁוּף וּמִבִּלְבּוּל הַדַּעַת, וְאַל יִדְוֶה לִבֵּנוּ וְאַל יֶחְשְׁכוּ עֵינֵינוּ. וְנִהְיֶה מְיֻשָּׁבִים בְּדַעְתֵּנוּ, וְתֵן בָּנוּ כֹּחַ וּבְרִיאוּת לַעֲבוֹדָתְךָ וְיִרְאָתֶךָ.

וְתַאֲרִיךְ יָמֵינוּ בַּטוֹב

Veta'arich yameinu battov
uvanne'imim, uvchol asher nifneh
naskil uvchol asher na'aseh
natzliach. Amen ken yehi ratzon.
Yehi chasdecha adonai aleinu
ka'asher yichalnu lach. Har'einu
adonai chasdecha v'yesh'acha
titten lanu. Va'ani bechasdecha
batachti yageil libbi bishu'atecha
ashirah ladonai ki gamal alai.
Hinneih el yeshu'ati evtach velo
efchad ki azzi v'zimrat yah adonai
vayhi li lishu'ah.

וּבַנְּעִימִים, וּבְכָל אֲשֶׁר נִפְנֶה
נַשְׂכִּיל וּבְכָל אֲשֶׁר נַעֲשֶׂה
נַצְלִיחַ. אָמֵן כֵּן יְהִי רָצוֹן.
יְהִי חַסְדְּךָ יְיָ עָלֵינוּ
כַּאֲשֶׁר יִחַלְנוּ לָךְ. הַרְאֵנוּ
יְיָ חַסְדֶּךָ וְיֶשְׁעֲךָ
תִּתֶּן לָנוּ. וַאֲנִי בְּחַסְדְּךָ
בָטַחְתִּי יָגֵל לִבִּי בִּישׁוּעָתֶךָ
אָשִׁירָה לַיְיָ כִּי גָמַל עָלָי.
הִנֵּה אֵל יְשׁוּעָתִי אֶבְטַח וְלֹא
אֶפְחָד כִּי עָזִּי וְזִמְרָת יָהּ יְיָ
וַיְהִי לִי לִישׁוּעָה.

Notes

_____
_____
_____
_____
_____
_____
_____
_____
_____
_____
_____
_____
_____

Prayers for the Deceased

In moments of loss and mourning, prayer is a deep source of comfort and connection. The following prayers help us navigate the pain of loss by reminding us of God's eternal companionship and the indelible bond we share with the departed. They help us honor and stay connected to our loved ones beyond their death.

Selected Psalms to be Recited in the Presence of the Deceased

Psalm 23

Psalm 23 is often recited at funerals as a source of comfort, hope, and solace for those who are grieving. Its words evoke a deep sense of trust and faith in God's guidance and protection, even in the most challenging times. Its imagery reassures us that, even in the face of death or profound loss, we are not alone. God is with us, providing comfort and sustenance.

A psalm of David. The Lord is my shepherd; I shall not want. He makes me lie down in green pastures; He leads me to water in places of repose; He renews my life; He guides me in right paths as befits His name. Though I walk through a valley of the shadow of death, I fear no evil, for You are with me; Your rod and Your staff—they comfort me. You spread a table for me in full view of my enemies; You anoint my head with oil; my drink is abundant. Only goodness and steadfast love shall pursue me all the days of my life, and I shall dwell in the house of the Lord for many long years.

Mizmor ledavid adonai ro'i lo echsar. Bin'ot deshe yarbitzeini al-mei menuchot yenahaleini. Nafshi yeshoveiv yancheini vema'gelei-tzedek lema'an shemo. Gam ki-eileich begei tzalmavet lo-ira ra ki-attah immadi

מִזְמוֹר לְדָוִד יְהֹוָה רֹעִי לֹא
אֶחְסָר: בִּנְאוֹת דֶּשֶׁא יַרְבִּיצֵנִי עַל־
מֵי מְנֻחוֹת יְנַהֲלֵנִי: נַפְשִׁי
יְשׁוֹבֵב יַנְחֵנִי בְמַעְגְּלֵי־
צֶדֶק לְמַעַן שְׁמוֹ: גַּם
כִּי־אֵלֵךְ בְּגֵיא צַלְמָוֶת לֹא־אִירָא רָע
כִּי־אַתָּה עִמָּדִי

shivtecha umish'antecha heimmah	שִׁבְטְךָ וּמִשְׁעַנְתֶּךָ הֵמָּה
yenachamuni. Ta'aroch lefanai	יְנַחֲמֻנִי: תַּעֲרֹךְ לְפָנַי
shulchan neged tzorerai dishanta	שֻׁלְחָן נֶגֶד צֹרְרָי דִּשַּׁנְתָּ
vashemen roshi kosi revayah. Ach	בַשֶּׁמֶן רֹאשִׁי כּוֹסִי רְוָיָה: אַךְ
tov vachesed yirdefuni kol-yemei	טוֹב וָחֶסֶד יִרְדְּפוּנִי כָּל־יְמֵי
chayyai veshavti beveit-adonai	חַיָּי וְשַׁבְתִּי בְּבֵית־יְהֹוָה
le'orech yamim.	לְאֹרֶךְ יָמִים:

Psalm 91

Psalm 91 offers comfort by affirming God's protection and presence, particularly during our deepest troubles. The promise 'I will be with him in distress' emphasizes that God's unwavering support accompanies us in our darkest hours. This psalm reminds us that not only do we find shelter under God's wing in this world, but our loved ones are sitting in His shelter in the afterlife as well.

O you who dwell in the shelter of the Most High and abide in the protection of Shaddai— I say of the Lord, my refuge and stronghold, my God in whom I trust, that He will save you from the fowler's trap, from the destructive plague. He will cover you with His pinions; you will find refuge under His wings; His fidelity is an encircling shield. You need not fear the terror by night, or the arrow that flies by day, the plague that stalks in the darkness, or the scourge that ravages at noon. A thousand may fall at your left side, ten thousand at your right, but it shall not reach you. You will see it with your eyes, you will witness the punishment of the wicked. Because you took the Lord—my refuge, the Most High— as your haven, no harm will befall you, no disease will touch your tent. For He will order His angels to guard you wherever you go. They will carry you in their hands lest you hurt your foot on a stone. You will tread on cubs and vipers; you will trample lions and asps. "Because he is devoted to Me I will deliver him; I will keep him safe, for he knows My name. When he calls on Me, I will answer him; I will be with him in distress; I will rescue him and make him honored; I will let him live to a ripe old age, and show him My salvation."

Yosheiv beseiter elyon betzeil	יֹשֵׁב בְּסֵתֶר עֶלְיוֹן בְּצֵל
shaddai yitlonan. Omar ladonai	שַׁדַּי יִתְלוֹנָן: אֹמַר לַיהוָה
machsi umetzudati elohai	מַחְסִי וּמְצוּדָתִי אֱלֹהַי
evtach-bo. Ki hu yatzilcha	אֶבְטַח־בּוֹ: כִּי הוּא יַצִּילְךָ
mippach yakush middever	מִפַּח יָקוּשׁ מִדֶּבֶר
havvot. Be'evrato yasech lach	הַוּוֹת: בְּאֶבְרָתוֹ יָסֶךְ לָךְ
vetachat-kenafav techseh	וְתַחַת־כְּנָפָיו תֶּחְסֶה
tzinnah vesocheirah amitto.	צִנָּה וְסֹחֵרָה אֲמִתּוֹ:
Lo-tira mippachad lai'lah	לֹא־תִירָא מִפַּחַד לָיְלָה
mecheitz ya'uf yomam. Middever	מֵחֵץ יָעוּף יוֹמָם: מִדֶּבֶר
ba'ofel yahaloch mikketev	בָּאֹפֶל יַהֲלֹךְ מִקֶּטֶב
yashud tzohorayim. Yippol	יָשׁוּד צָהֳרָיִם: יִפֹּל
mitziddecha elef urevavah	מִצִּדְּךָ אֶלֶף וּרְבָבָה
miminecha eleicha lo yiggash.	מִימִינֶךָ אֵלֶיךָ לֹא יִגָּשׁ:
Rak be'eineicha tabbit veshillumat	רַק בְּעֵינֶיךָ תַבִּיט וְשִׁלֻּמַת
resha'im tir'eh. Ki-attah adonai	רְשָׁעִים תִּרְאֶה: כִּי־אַתָּה יְהוָה
machsi elyon samta me'onecha.	מַחְסִי עֶלְיוֹן שַׂמְתָּ מְעוֹנֶךָ:
Lo-te'unneh eleicha ra'ah	לֹא־תְאֻנֶּה אֵלֶיךָ רָעָה
venega lo-yikrav be'oholecha.	וְנֶגַע לֹא־יִקְרַב בְּאָהֳלֶךָ:
Ki mal'achav yetzavveh-lach	כִּי מַלְאָכָיו יְצַוֶּה־לָּךְ
lishmorcha bechol-derachecha.	לִשְׁמָרְךָ בְּכָל־דְּרָכֶיךָ:
Al-kappayim yissa'uncha pen-	עַל־כַּפַּיִם יִשָּׂאוּנְךָ פֶּן־
tiggof ba'even raglecha. Al-	תִּגֹּף בָּאֶבֶן רַגְלֶךָ: עַל־
shachal vafeten tidroch tirmos	שַׁחַל וָפֶתֶן תִּדְרֹךְ תִּרְמֹס
kefir vetannin. Ki vi chashak	כְּפִיר וְתַנִּין: כִּי בִי חָשַׁק

va'afalletehu asaggevehu ki-yada shemi. Yikra'eini ve'e'eneihu immo-anochi vetzarah achalletzeihu va'achabbedeihu. Orech yamim asbi'eihu ve'ar'eihu bishu'ati.

וַאֲפַלְּטֵהוּ אֲשַׂגְּבֵהוּ
כִּי־יָדַע שְׁמִי: יִקְרָאֵנִי
וְאֶעֱנֵהוּ עִמּוֹ־אָנֹכִי בְצָרָה
אֲחַלְּצֵהוּ וַאֲכַבְּדֵהוּ:
אֹרֶךְ יָמִים אַשְׂבִּיעֵהוּ וְאַרְאֵהוּ
בִּישׁוּעָתִי:

Notes

_____

_____

_____

_____

_____

_____

_____

_____

_____

_____

_____

_____

_____

_____

_____

_____

_____

The Memorial Prayer for a Deceased Relative

*Y*IZKOR, MEANING "MAY God remember," is a memorial prayer for those who have departed. Though it is a short prayer, it has a deep spiritual impact on the soul of the departed, as well as an emotional impact on those who recite it. By reciting *Yizkor*, we renew our bond with our loved ones and elevate their souls.

The *Yizkor* prayer asks God to remember the souls of those who have passed away, and we honor the deceased by making a personal commitment to give charity in their memory. *Yizkor* is also a time for personal reflection and commitment to self-improvement as a source of merit for the departed.

Yizkor is traditionally recited in synagogues following the Torah reading on the last day of Passover, on the Feast of Weeks, on the Eighth Day of Assembly and on the Day of Atonement, but it can be recited at other times as well.

Yizkor for a father:

*Remember, God, the soul of my father, my teacher (**insert the name of your father, son of the name of his father**), who went to his world, because I will - without making a vow - give charity for him. In recompense for this, let his soul be bound with the Binding of life (God), with the soul of Abraham, Isaac and Jacob, Sarah, Rebecca, Rachel and Leah, and with the other righteous men and women in the Garden of Eden. And let us say, Amen.*

Yizkor elohim nishmat avi mori
(insert *father's name*, ben
his father's name) shehalach
le'olamo, ba'avur she'ettein
beli neder tzedakah ba'ado.
Bischar zeh tehei nafsho tzerurah
bitzror hachayyim im nishmat
avraham yitzchak veya'akov,
sarah rivkah rachel vele'ah, ve'im
she'ar tzaddikim vetzidkaniyyot
shebbegan eiden. Venomar
amen.

יִזְכֹּר אֱלֹהִים נִשְׁמַת אָבִי מוֹרִי
(שם האב בן
שם אביו) שֶׁהָלַךְ
לְעוֹלָמוֹ, בַּעֲבוּר שֶׁאֶתֵּן
בְּלִי נֶדֶר צְדָקָה בַּעֲדוֹ.
בִּשְׂכַר זֶה תְּהֵא נַפְשׁוֹ צְרוּרָה
בִּצְרוֹר הַחַיִּים עִם נִשְׁמַת
אַבְרָהָם יִצְחָק וְיַעֲקֹב,
שָׂרָה רִבְקָה רָחֵל וְלֵאָה, וְעִם
שְׁאָר צַדִּיקִים וְצִדְקָנִיּוֹת
שֶׁבְּגַן עֵדֶן. וְנֹאמַר
אָמֵן.

Yizkor for a mother:

*Remember, God, the soul of my mother, my teacher (**insert the
name of your mother**, daughter of **the name of her father**), who
went to her world, because I will - without making a vow - give
charity for her. In recompense for this, let her soul be bound with
the Binding of life (God), with the soul of Abraham, Isaac and Jacob,
Sarah, Rebecca, Rachel and Leah, and with the other righteous
men and women in the Garden of Eden. And let us say, Amen.*

Yizkor elohim nishmat immi morati
(*mother's name*, bat *her father's
name*) shehalechah le'olamah,
ba'avur she'ettein beli neder
tzedakah ba'adah. Bischar zeh
tehei nafshah tzerurah bitzror
hachayyim im nishmat avraham
yitzchak veya'akov,

יִזְכֹּר אֱלֹהִים נִשְׁמַת אִמִּי
מוֹרָתִי (שם האם בת
שם אביה) שֶׁהָלְכָה
לְעוֹלָמָהּ, בַּעֲבוּר שֶׁאֶתֵּן בְּלִי
נֶדֶר צְדָקָה בַּעֲדָהּ. בִּשְׂכַר
זֶה תְּהֵא נַפְשָׁהּ צְרוּרָה
בִּצְרוֹר הַחַיִּים עִם נִשְׁמַת
אַבְרָהָם יִצְחָק וְיַעֲקֹב,

sarah rivkah rachel velei'ah, ve'im she'ar tzaddikim vetzidkaniyyot shebbegan eiden. Venomar amen.

שָׂרָה רִבְקָה רָחֵל וְלֵאָה, וְעִם שְׁאָר צַדִּיקִים וְצִדְקָנִיּוֹת שֶׁבְּגַן עֵדֶן. וְנֹאמַר אָמֵן.

Yizkor for a relative:

*Remember, God, the soul of (**insert the name of the deceased** son or daughter of **the name of the deceased's father**), who went to his/her world, because I will - without making a vow - give charity for him/her. In recompense for this, let his/her soul be bound with the Binding of life (God), with the soul of Abraham, Isaac and Jacob, Sarah, Rebecca, Rachel and Leah, and with the other righteous men and women in the Garden of Eden. And let us say, Amen.*

Yizkor elohim nishmat (zekenai uzekenotai, dodai vedodotai, achai ve'achyotai, banai uvenotai, ba'ali, ishti) *(name of the deceased* ben/bat *their father's name)* shehalach le'olamo, ba'avur she'ettein beli neder tzedakah ba'ado. Bischar zeh tehe nafsho tzerurah bitzror hachayyim im nishmat avraham yitzchak veya'akov, sarah rivkah rachel vele'ah, ve'im she'ar tzaddikim vetzidkaniyyot shebbegan eiden. Venomar amen.

יִזְכֹּר אֱלֹהִים נִשְׁמַת (זְקֵנַי וּזְקֵנוֹתַי, דּוֹדַי וְדוֹדוֹתַי, אָחַי וְאַחְיוֹתַי, בָּנַי וּבְנוֹתַי, בַּעֲלִי, אִשְׁתִּי) (שם הנפטר בן שם אביו) שֶׁהָלַךְ לְעוֹלָמוֹ, בַּעֲבוּר שֶׁאֶתֵּן בְּלִי נֶדֶר צְדָקָה בַּעֲדוֹ. בִּשְׂכַר זֶה תְּהֵא נַפְשׁוֹ צְרוּרָה בִּצְרוֹר הַחַיִּים עִם נִשְׁמַת אַבְרָהָם יִצְחָק וְיַעֲקֹב, שָׂרָה רִבְקָה רָחֵל וְלֵאָה, וְעִם שְׁאָר צַדִּיקִים וְצִדְקָנִיּוֹת שֶׁבְּגַן עֵדֶן. וְנֹאמַר אָמֵן.

Mourner's Kaddish
Recited Following the Death
of a Close Relative

THE MOURNER'S KADDISH is an Aramaic prayer said follow-ing the death of a close family member. The prayer itself does not mention death, but rather proclaims the greatness of God. It is recited by a relative as a source of merit for the deceased, and demonstrates that their faith endures despite their loss.

Exalted and sanctified be His great Name (Amen)
in the world which He created according to His will and may He rule His kingdom. In your lifetime and in your days, and in the lifetime of the entire House of Israel, speedily and in the near future — and say Amen.
May His great Name be blessed forever and for all eternity.
Blessed and praised, glorified, and exalted and uplifted, honored and elevated and extolled be the Name of the Holy One, blessed is He;
above all the blessings and hymns, praises and consolations which we utter in the world— and say Amen.
May there be abundant peace from heaven and a good life for us and for all Israel, — and say Amen.
He Who makes peace in His high heavens may He, in His mercy, make peace for us and for all Israel, — and say Amen.

Yitgaddal veyitkaddash shemeih　　　　　יִתְגַּדַּל וְיִתְקַדַּשׁ שְׁמֵהּ

rabba (amein)　　　　　　　　　　　　　רַבָּא (אָמֵן)

Be'alema di-vera chir'uteih　　　　　　כְּעָלְמָא דִּי־בְרָא כִרְעוּתֵהּ

veyamlich malchuteih	וְיַמְלִיךְ מַלְכוּתֵהּ
bechayyeichon uveyomeichon	בְּחַיֵּיכוֹן וּבְיוֹמֵיכוֹן
uvechayyei dechol-beit yisra'el	וּבְחַיֵּי דְכָל־בֵּית יִשְׂרָאֵל
ba'agala uvizman kariv ve'imru	בַּעֲגָלָא וּבִזְמַן קָרִיב וְאִמְרוּ
amein:	אָמֵן:
Yehei shemeih rabba mevarach	יְהֵא שְׁמֵהּ רַבָּא מְבָרַךְ
le'alam ule'alemei alemayya	לְעָלַם וּלְעָלְמֵי עָלְמַיָּא
yitbarach veyishtabbach	יִתְבָּרַךְ וְיִשְׁתַּבַּח
veyitpa'ar veyitromam veyitnassei	וְיִתְפָּאַר וְיִתְרוֹמַם וְיִתְנַשֵּׂא
veyithaddar veyit'alleh veyithallal	וְיִתְהַדָּר וְיִתְעַלֶּה וְיִתְהַלָּל
shemeih dekudesha berich hu	שְׁמֵהּ דְּקוּדְשָׁא בְּרִיךְ הוּא
Le'eilla min-kol birchata veshirata	לְעֵלָּא מִן־כָּל־בִּרְכָתָא וְשִׁירָתָא
tushbechata venechamata	תֻּשְׁבְּחָתָא וְנֶחָמָתָא
da'amiran be'alema ve'imru amen:	דַּאֲמִירָן בְּעָלְמָא וְאִמְרוּ אָמֵן:
Yehei shelama rabba min-	יְהֵא שְׁלָמָא רַבָּא מִן־
shemayya vechayyim aleinu ve'al-	שְׁמַיָּא וְחַיִּים עָלֵינוּ וְעַל־
kol-yisra'eil ve'imru amen: Oseh	כָּל־יִשְׂרָאֵל וְאִמְרוּ אָמֵן:עֹשֶׂה
shalom bimromav hu ya'aseh	שָׁלוֹם בִּמְרוֹמָיו הוּא יַעֲשֶׂה
shalom aleinu ve'al kol yisra'eil	שָׁלוֹם עָלֵינוּ וְעַל כָּל יִשְׂרָאֵל
ve'imru amein:	וְאִמְרוּ אָמֵן:

Notes

_____

_____

_____

_____

_____

_____

Prayers for Sustenance

In our quest for sustenance and financial security, we must recognize that God is the ultimate sustainer. While we must do our part to achieve financial stability, turning to God is equally important. As we turn to God in search of material sustenance, the following prayers also encourage us to deepen our reliance and faith in the Divine as the Source of all.

Prayer for Livelihood

THE FOLLOWING PRAYER for physical sustenance was written by Rabbi Shlomo Alkabetz (1505-1584), one of the great Jewish kabbalists of the 16th century. This prayer acknowledges God as the ultimate sustainer of all creatures, from the most majestic to the smallest, emphasizing that no other being, angelic or otherwise, can provide in the way God does.

You are the God who nourishes everything, from the horns of wild oxen to the eggs of lice. No angel or minister has the power to provide and sustain Your creatures. As written by your servant David: "The eyes of all look towards You, and You give them their food in due time. You open Your hand and satisfy the desire of every living thing." And it is written: "He gives bread to all flesh, for His mercy endures forever." This key is in Your hand, to refine and purify humans so that they may trust in You and know that there is no savior besides You.

Attah ha'eil hazzan mikkarnei	אַתָּה הָאֵל הַזָּן מִקַּרְנֵי
re'eimim ad beitzei kinnim,	רְאֵמִים עַד בֵּיצֵי כִּנִּים,
ve'ein beyad shum mal'ach	וְאֵין בְּיַד שׁוּם מַלְאָךְ
vesar lazun ulefarneis ulechalkeil	וְשַׂר לָזוּן וּלְפַרְנֵס וּלְכַלְכֵּל
kalkalatecha, kakkatuv al yedei	כַּלְכָּלָתֶךָ, כַּכָּתוּב עַל יְדֵי
david avdecha: einei chol eleicha	דָוִד עַבְדֶּךָ: עֵינֵי כֹל אֵלֶיךָ
yesabbeiru, ve'attah notein lahem	יְשַׂבֵּרוּ, וְאַתָּה נוֹתֵן לָהֶם
et ochlam be'itto: potei'ach et	אֶת אָכְלָם בְּעִתּוֹ: פּוֹתֵחַ אֶת
yadecha, umashbia' lechol chai	יָדֶךָ, וּמַשְׂבִּיעַ לְכָל חַי
ratzon: uchetiv: notein lechem	רָצוֹן: וּכְתִיב: נֹתֵן לֶחֶם

lechol basar, ki le'olam chasdo:
umafteach zeh hu beyadecha
letzareif ulelabbein benei adam
lesheyyivtechu becha veyeide'u ki
moshia' ein biltecha:

לְכָל בָּשָׂר, כִּי לְעוֹלָם חַסְדּוֹ:
וּמַפְתֵּחַ זֶה הוּא בְּיָדֶךָ
לְצָרֵף וּלְלַבֵּן בְּנֵי אָדָם
לְשֶׁיִּבְטְחוּ בָּךְ וְיֵדְעוּ כִּי
מוֹשִׁיעַ אֵין בִּלְתֶּךָ:

Notes

_____

_____

_____

_____

_____

_____

_____

_____

_____

_____

_____

_____

_____

_____

_____

_____

_____

_____

Prayer to be Saved from Debts and Loans

Rabbi Nathan of Breslov (1780-1844) was the main disciple and scribe of Rabbi Nachman of Breslov, the founder of the Breslov Hasidic dynasty. He wrote the following prayer as an earnest plea to God for relief from financial distress. With this prayer, we seek God's help in overcoming dependency on others and in rectifying past wrongdoings, including theft.

Master of the Universe, You know the lack of livelihood at this time when "the strength of the bearer has faltered," for our lives hang in the balance, and we do not know any way to obtain a livelihood. We rely solely on You, for from whom else shall I ask for my bread, my sustenance, and all my many needs? Surely only from You, who provides and sustains everything from the horns of the wild oxen to the eggs of lice. Have mercy on me and save me, and provide me with sustenance generously from under Your wide and full hand, and do not make me dependent on the gifts of flesh and blood or on their loans. And help me to clear all the debts that I already owe, and from now on save me that I may not come to any debt or loan at all. Be my helper so that I may soon rectify the damage of all the thefts that are in my hands from my youth until this day. And may I merit to return all the thefts I have stolen, or the oppression that I have committed, whether inadvertently or intentionally, whether under duress or willingly. And all kinds of monetary disputes that remain in my hands, any money of my fellow that is in my possession due to any mistake or concealment from any transaction, debt, and the like, whether I still remember it or have forgotten it, may I merit to clear and pay it back to its owners quickly and easily. And in Your mercy, grant me much money so that I can fulfill my obligation to remove from anyone whose money or possessions I have touched in any way in the world. And if, God forbid, I have in my possession any theft or debt that I am not aware of myself to whom I have stolen, help me in Your great mercy, that I may use them for public needs, as You commanded us through Your holy sages, so that I may quickly, in my life, rectify and return all the thefts and debts that are in my hands. For You know the severity of the prohibition of theft, which is considered as if he steals his own life and the lives of his sons and daughters, and as if he violated another man's wife. O merciful God, have pity and compassion on my soul, and help me rectify the damage of all the thefts and debts that are in my hands, and broaden my hand, and help me and grant me to give much charity to many worthy poor people, so that I may rectify through this the damage of the thefts that are in my hands through desire, which I coveted and desired from others until I stole it through this. Please, Lord, allow me to rectify this through charity.

Ribbono shel olam, attah yodei'a	רִבּוֹנוֹ שֶׁל עוֹלָם, אַתָּה
chesron happarnasah ba'eit	יוֹדֵעַ חֶסְרוֹן הַפַּרְנָסָה
hazzot asher "kashal koach	בָּעֵת הַזֹּאת אֲשֶׁר "כָּשַׁל
hassabbal," ki chayyeinu teluyim	כֹּחַ הַסַּבָּל", כִּי חַיֵּינוּ
minneged, ve'ein anu yode'im	תְּלוּיִם מִנֶּגֶד, וְאֵין אָנוּ
shum derech eich lehassig	יוֹדְעִים שׁוּם דֶּרֶךְ אֵיךְ
parnasah, ki im aleicha levad	לְהַשִׂיג פַּרְנָסָה, כִּי אִם עָלֶיךָ
anu nish'anim, ki mimmi esh'al	לְבַד אָנוּ נִשְׁעָנִים, כִּי מִמִּי
lachmi ufarnasati vechol tzerachai	אֶשְׁאַל לַחְמִי וּפַרְנָסָתִי וְכָל
hammerubbim me'od, halo	צְרָכַי הַמְרֻבִּים מְאֹד,
mimmecha levad, asher attah	הֲלֹא מִמְּךָ לְבַד, אֲשֶׁר
mefarnes umechalkeil	אַתָּה מְפַרְנֵס וּמְכַלְכֵּל

mikkarnei re'emim ad beitzei
chinnim. Chamol alai vehoshi'eini,
veten li parnasah berevach
mittachat yadecha harechavah
vehammelei'ah, ve'al tatzricheini
lo lidei mattenat basar vadam
velo lidei halva'atam. Ve'azereini
lesallek kol hachovot she'ani
chayyav mikkevar, umei'attah
tatzileini shello avo lidei shum
chov vehalva'ah kelal. Vetihyeh
be'ezri she'ezkeh meheirah
letakkein pegam kol haggezeilot
shebbeyadi me'odi ad hayyom
hazzeh. Ve'ezkeh lehashiv et
kol haggezeilot asher gazalti, o
et ha'oshek asher ashakti, bein
beshogeg bein bemeizid bein
be'ones bein beratzon. Vechol
minei sichsuchim be'iskei mamon,
shennish'ar beyadi eizeh mamon
shel chaverai al-yedei eizeh ta'ut
veha'lamah me'eizeh massa
umattan vechov vechaddomeh,
hen mah she'ani zocher adayin,
hen mah shennishkach mimmenni,
hakkol ezkeh lesalleik uleshalleim
leva'aleihem chish kal meheirah.
Vetashpia' li berachamecha
mamon harbeih, be'ofen
she'ezkeh latzeit yedei chovati
lesalleik lechol mi shennaga'ti
bemamono vachafatzav shum

מִקַּרְנֵי רְאֵמִים עַד בֵּיצֵי
כִנִּים. חֲמֹל עָלַי וְהוֹשִׁיעֵנִי,
וְתֶן לִי פַּרְנָסָה בְּרֶוַח
מִתַּחַת יָדְךָ הָרְחָבָה
וְהַמְלֵאָה, וְאַל תַּצְרִיכֵנִי
לֹא לִידֵי מַתְּנַת בָּשָׂר וָדָם
וְלֹא לִידֵי הַלְוָאָתָם. וְעָזְרֵנִי
לְסַלֵּק כָּל הַחוֹבוֹת שֶׁאֲנִי
חַיָּב מִכְּבָר, וּמֵעַתָּה
תַּצִּילֵנִי שֶׁלֹּא אָבֹא לִידֵי שׁוּם
חוֹב וְהַלְוָאָה כְּלָל. וְתִהְיֶה
בְּעֶזְרִי שֶׁאֶזְכֶּה מְהֵרָה
לְתַקֵּן פְּגַם כָּל הַגְּזֵלוֹת
שֶׁבְּיָדִי מְעוֹדִי עַד הַיּוֹם
הַזֶּה. וְאֶזְכֶּה לְהָשִׁיב אֶת
כָּל הַגְּזֵלוֹת אֲשֶׁר גָּזַלְתִּי, אוֹ
אֶת הָעֹשֶׁק אֲשֶׁר עָשַׁקְתִּי, בֵּין
בְּשׁוֹגֵג בֵּין בְּמֵזִיד בֵּין
בְּאֹנֶס בֵּין בְּרָצוֹן. וְכָל
מִינֵי סְכְסוּכִים בְּעִסְקֵי מָמוֹן,
שֶׁנִּשְׁאָר בְּיָדִי אֵיזֶה מָמוֹן
שֶׁל חֲבֵרַי עַל-יְדֵי אֵיזֶה טָעוּת
וְהַעְלָמָה מֵאֵיזֶה מַשָּׂא
וּמַתָּן וְחוֹב וְכַדּוֹמֶה,
הֵן מַה שֶׁאֲנִי זוֹכֵר עֲדַיִן,
הֵן מַה שֶׁנִּשְׁכַּח מִמֶּנִּי,
הַכֹּל אֶזְכֶּה לְסַלֵּק וּלְשַׁלֵּם
לְבַעֲלֵיהֶם חִישׁ קַל מְהֵרָה.
וְתַשְׁפִּיעַ לִי בְּרַחֲמֶיךָ
מָמוֹן הַרְבֵּה, בְּאֹפֶן
שֶׁאֶזְכֶּה לָצֵאת יְדֵי חוֹבָתִי
לְסַלֵּק לְכָל מִי שֶׁנָּגַעְתִּי
בְּמָמוֹנוֹ וַחֲפָצָיו שׁוּם

צַד נְגִיעָה בָּעוֹלָם. וְאִם חַס
וְשָׁלוֹם יֵשׁ בְּיָדִי אֵיזֶה
גְּזֵלָה וָחוֹב שֶׁאֵינִי יוֹדֵעַ
בְּעַצְמִי לְמִי גָזָלְתִּי, תַּעַזְרֵנִי
בְּרַחֲמֶיךָ הָרַבִּים,
שֶׁאֶזְכֶּה לַעֲשׂוֹת מֵהֶם
צָרְכֵי רַבִּים, כַּאֲשֶׁר
צִוִּיתָנוּ עַל־יְדֵי חֲכָמֶיךָ
הַקְּדוֹשִׁים, בְּאֹפֶן שֶׁאֶזְכֶּה
מְהֵרָה בְּחַיַּי לְתַקֵּן
וּלְהַחֲזִיר כָּל הַגְּזֵלוֹת
וְהַחוֹבוֹת שֶׁבְּיָדִי. כִּי
אַתָּה יוֹדֵעַ חֹמֶר אִסּוּר
גְּזֵלָה שֶׁנֶּחְשָׁב כְּאִלּוּ
גּוֹזֵל נַפְשׁוֹ וְנֶפֶשׁ בָּנָיו
וּבְנוֹתָיו, וּכְאִלּוּ בָּא עַל אֵשֶׁת
אִישׁ. מָלֵא רַחֲמִים, חוּס
וַחֲמֹל עַל נַפְשִׁי, וְעָזְרֵנִי
לְתַקֵּן פְּגַם כָּל הַגְּזֵלוֹת
וְהַחוֹבוֹת שֶׁבְּיָדִי, וְתַרְחִיב
אֶת יָדִי, וְתַעַזְרֵנִי וּתְזַכֵּנִי
לִתֵּן צְדָקָה הַרְבֵּה לַעֲנִיִּים
הֲגוּנִים הַרְבֵּה, בְּאֹפֶן
שֶׁאֶזְכֶּה לְתַקֵּן עַל־יְדֵי־זֶה
פְּגַם הַגְּזֵלוֹת שֶׁבְּיָדִי
עַל־יְדֵי חֶמְדָּה, מַה שֶּׁהָיִיתִי
חוֹמֵד וּמִתְאַוֶּה אֶת שֶׁל
חֲבֵרִי, עַד שֶׁגָּזַלְתִּי אוֹתוֹ עַל־
יְדֵי־זֶה. אָנָּא יְהֹוָה, זַכֵּנִי
לְתַקֵּן זֹאת עַל־יְדֵי צְדָקָה.

tzad negi'ah ba'olam. Ve'im chas
veshalom yesh beyadi eizeh
gezeilah vachov she'eini yodea'
be'atzmi lemi gazalti, ta'azreini
berachamecha harabbim,
she'ezkeh la'asot meihem
tzarechei rabbim, ka'asher
tzivvitanu al-yedei chachameicha
hakkedoshim, be'ofen she'ezkeh
meheirah bechayyai letakken
ulehachazir kol haggezeilot
vehachovot shebbeyadi. Ki
attah yodea' chomer issur
gezelah shennechshav ke'illu
gozel nafsho venefesh banav
uvenotav, uche'illu ba al eshet
ish. Malei rachamim, chus
vachamol al nafshi, ve'azereini
letakken pegam kol haggezelot
vehachovot shebbeyadi, vetarchiv
et yadi, veta'azreni utezakkeini
litten tzedakah harbeih la'aniyyim
hagunim harbeih, be'ofen
she'ezkeh letakkein al-yedei-zeh
pegam haggezelot shebbeyadi
al-yedei chemdah, mah shehayiti
chomeid umit'avveh et shel
chaveiri, ad sheggazalti oto al-
yedei-zeh. Anna adonai, zakkeini
letakkein zot al-yedei tzedakah.

Psalms to Recite When Looking for Work or Greater Financial Stability

Psalm 104

Psalms 104 celebrates the majesty and providence of God in the natural world, showcasing His wisdom and care in the creation and sustenance of all life. For those seeking a livelihood, this psalm is a powerful reminder of God's role as the ultimate provider. It invites us to trust that He will provide for those who depend on Him for their sustenance and well-being.

Bless the Lord, O my soul; O Lord, my God, You are very great; You are clothed in glory and majesty, wrapped in a robe of light; You spread the heavens like a tent cloth. He sets the rafters of His lofts in the waters, makes the clouds His chariot, moves on the wings of the wind. He makes the winds His messengers, fiery flames His servants. He established the earth on its foundations, so that it shall never totter. You made the deep cover it as a garment; the waters stood above the mountains. They fled at Your blast, rushed away at the sound of Your thunder, —mountains rising, valleys sinking— to the place You established for them. You set bounds they must not pass so that they never again cover the earth. You make springs gush forth in torrents; they make their way between the hills, giving drink to all the wild beasts; the wild asses slake their thirst. The birds of the sky dwell beside them and sing among the foliage. You water the mountains from Your lofts; the earth is sated from the fruit of Your work. You make the grass grow for the cattle, and herbage for man's labor, that he may get food out of the earth— wine that cheers the hearts of men, oil that makes the face shine, and bread that sustains man's life. The trees of the Lord drink their fill, the cedars of Lebanon, His own planting, where birds make their nests; the stork has her home in the junipers. The high mountains are for wild goats; the crags are a refuge for rock-badgers. He made the moon to mark the seasons; the sun knows when to set. You bring on darkness and it is night, when all the beasts of the forests stir. The lions roar for prey, seeking their food from God. When the sun rises, they come home and couch in their dens. Man then goes out to his work, to his labor until the evening. How many are the things You have made, O Lord ; You have made them all with wisdom; the earth is full of Your creations. There is the sea, vast and wide, with its creatures beyond number, living things, small and great. There go the ships, and Leviathan that You formed to sport with. All of them look to You to give them their food when it is due. Give it to them, they gather it up; open Your hand, they are well satisfied; hide Your face, they are terrified; take away their breath, they perish and turn again into dust; send back Your breath, they are created, and You renew the face of the earth. May the glory of the Lord endure forever; may the Lord rejoice in His works! He looks at the earth and it trembles; He touches the mountains and they smoke. I will sing to the Lord as long as I live; all my life I will chant hymns to my God. May my prayer be pleasing to Him; I will rejoice in the Lord . May sinners disappear from the earth, and the wicked be no more. Bless the Lord, O my soul. Halleluyah.

Barechi nafshi et-adonai adonai	בָּרְכִי נַפְשִׁי אֶת־יְהֹוָה יְהֹוָה
elohai gadalta me'od hod vehadar	אֱלֹהַי גָּדַלְתָּ מְּאֹד הוֹד
lavasheta. Oteh-or kassalmah	וְהָדָר לָבָשְׁתָּ: עֹטֶה־אוֹר
noteh shamayim	כַּשַּׂלְמָה נוֹטֶה שָׁמַיִם
kayyeri'ah. Hamkareh vammayim	כַּיְרִיעָה: הַמְקָרֶה בַמַּיִם
aliyyotav hassam-avim rechuvo	עֲלִיּוֹתָיו הַשָּׂם־עָבִים רְכוּבוֹ

hammehalleich al-kanfei- ruach. Oseh mal'achav ruchot mesharetav eish loheit. Yasad- eretz al-mechoneha bal-timmot olam va'ed. Tehom kallevush kissito al-harim ya'amdu mayim. Min-ga'aratecha yenusun min- kol ra'amcha yechafeizun. Ya'alu harim yeiredu veka'ot el-mekom zeh yasadta lahem. Gevul-samta bal-ya'avorun bal- yeshuvun lechassot ha'aretz. Hammeshallei'ach ma'yanim bannechalim bein harim yehalleichun. Yashku kol-chayto sadai yishberu fera'im tzema'am. Aleihem of-hashamayim yishkon mibbein ofayim yittenu-kol. Mashkeh harim mei'aliyyotav mipperi ma'aseicha tisba ha'aretz. Matzmiach chatzir labbeheimah ve'eisev la'avodat ha'adam lehotzi lechem min-ha'aretz. Veyayin yesammach levav-enosh lehatzhil panim mishamen velechem levav-enosh yis'ad. Yisbe'u atzei adonai arzei levanon asher nata. Asher-sham tzipporim yekanneinu chasidah beroshim beitah. Harim haggevohim layye'eilim sela'im machseh lashfannim. Asah yarei'ach lemo'adim shemesh yada mevo'o. Tashet-	הַמְהַלֵּךְ עַל־כַּנְפֵי־ רוּחַ: עֹשֶׂה מַלְאָכָיו רוּחוֹת מְשָׁרְתָיו אֵשׁ לֹהֵט: יָסַד־ אֶרֶץ עַל־מְכוֹנֶיהָ בַּל־תִּמּוֹט עוֹלָם וָעֶד: תְּהוֹם כַּלְּבוּשׁ כִּסִּיתוֹ עַל־הָרִים יַעַמְדוּ מָיִם: מִן־גַּעֲרָתְךָ יְנוּסוּן מִן־ קוֹל רַעַמְךָ יֵחָפֵזוּן: יַעֲלוּ הָרִים יֵרְדוּ בְקָעוֹת אֶל־מְקוֹם זֶה יָסַדְתָּ לָהֶם: גְּבוּל־שַׂמְתָּ בַּל־יַעֲבֹרוּן בַּל־ יְשׁוּבוּן לְכַסּוֹת הָאָרֶץ: הַמְשַׁלֵּחַ מַעְיָנִים בַּנְּחָלִים בֵּין הָרִים יְהַלֵּכוּן: יַשְׁקוּ כָּל־חַיְתוֹ שָׂדָי יִשְׁבְּרוּ פְרָאִים צְמָאָם: עֲלֵיהֶם עוֹף־הַשָּׁמַיִם יִשְׁכּוֹן מִבֵּין עֳפָאִים יִתְּנוּ־קוֹל: מַשְׁקֶה הָרִים מֵעֲלִיּוֹתָיו מִפְּרִי מַעֲשֶׂיךָ תִּשְׂבַּע הָאָרֶץ: מַצְמִיחַ חָצִיר לַבְּהֵמָה וְעֵשֶׂב לַעֲבֹדַת הָאָדָם לְהוֹצִיא לֶחֶם מִן־הָאָרֶץ: וְיַיִן יְשַׂמַּח לְבַב־אֱנוֹשׁ לְהַצְהִיל פָּנִים מִשָּׁמֶן וְלֶחֶם לְבַב־אֱנוֹשׁ יִסְעָד: יִשְׂבְּעוּ עֲצֵי יְהוָה אַרְזֵי לְבָנוֹן אֲשֶׁר נָטָע: אֲשֶׁר־שָׁם צִפֳּרִים יְקַנֵּנוּ חֲסִידָה בְּרוֹשִׁים בֵּיתָהּ: הָרִים הַגְּבֹהִים לַיְּעֵלִים סְלָעִים מַחְסֶה לַשְׁפַנִּים: עָשָׂה יָרֵחַ לְמוֹעֲדִים שֶׁמֶשׁ יָדַע מְבוֹאוֹ: תָּשֶׁת־

choshech vihi laylah bo-tirmos
kol-chayto-ya'ar. Hakkefirim
sho'agim lattaref ulevakkeish
me'el ochlam. Tizrach hashemesh
yei'aseifun ve'el-me'onotam
yirbatzun. Yeitzei adam lefo'alo
vela'avodato adei-arev. Mah-
rabbu ma'asecha adonai kullam
bechochmah asita male'ah
ha'aretz kinyanecha. Zeh hayyam
gadol urechav yadayim sham-
remes ve'ein mispar chayyot
ketannot im-gedolot. Sham
oniyyot yehalleichun livyatan
zeh-yatzarta lesacheik-bo. Kullam
eilecha yesabbeirun latet ochlam
be'itto. Tittein lahem yilkotun
tiftach yadecha yisbe'un tov. Tastir
panecha yibbaheilun tosef rucham
yigva'un ve'el-afaram yeshuvun.
Teshallach ruchacha yibbarei'un
utechaddeish penei adamah. Yehi
chevod adonai le'olam yismach
adonai bema'asav. Hammabbit
la'aretz vattir'ad yigga beharim
veye'eshanu. Ashirah ladonai
bechayyai azammerah leilohai
be'odi. Ye'erav alav sichi anochi
esmach badonai. Yittammu
chatta'im min-ha'aretz uresha'im
od einam barechi nafshi et-adonai
hallu-yah.

חֹשֶׁךְ וִיהִי לָיְלָה בּוֹ־תִרְמֹשׂ
כָּל־חַיְתוֹ־יָעַר: הַכְּפִירִים
שֹׁאֲגִים לַטָּרֶף וּלְבַקֵּשׁ
מֵאֵל אָכְלָם: תִּזְרַח הַשֶּׁמֶשׁ
יֵאָסֵפוּן וְאֶל־מְעוֹנֹתָם
יִרְבָּצוּן: יֵצֵא אָדָם לְפָעֳלוֹ
וְלַעֲבֹדָתוֹ עֲדֵי־עָרֶב: מָה־
רַבּוּ מַעֲשֶׂיךָ יְהוָה כֻּלָּם
בְּחָכְמָה עָשִׂיתָ מָלְאָה
הָאָרֶץ קִנְיָנֶךָ: זֶה הַיָּם
גָּדוֹל וּרְחַב יָדָיִם שָׁם־
רֶמֶשׂ וְאֵין מִסְפָּר חַיּוֹת
קְטַנּוֹת עִם־גְּדֹלוֹת: שָׁם
אֳנִיּוֹת יְהַלֵּכוּן לִוְיָתָן
זֶה־יָצַרְתָּ לְשַׂחֶק־בּוֹ: כֻּלָּם
אֵלֶיךָ יְשַׂבֵּרוּן לָתֵת אָכְלָם
בְּעִתּוֹ: תִּתֵּן לָהֶם יִלְקֹטוּן
תִּפְתַּח יָדְךָ יִשְׂבְּעוּן טוֹב: תַּסְתִּיר
פָּנֶיךָ יִבָּהֵלוּן תֹּסֵף רוּחָם
יִגְוָעוּן וְאֶל־עֲפָרָם יְשׁוּבוּן:
תְּשַׁלַּח רוּחֲךָ יִבָּרֵאוּן
וּתְחַדֵּשׁ פְּנֵי אֲדָמָה: יְהִי
כְבוֹד יְהוָה לְעוֹלָם יִשְׂמַח
יְהוָה בְּמַעֲשָׂיו: הַמַּבִּיט
לָאָרֶץ וַתִּרְעָד יִגַּע בֶּהָרִים
וְיֶעֱשָׁנוּ: אָשִׁירָה לַיהוָה
בְּחַיָּי אֲזַמְּרָה לֵאלֹהַי
בְּעוֹדִי: יֶעֱרַב עָלָיו שִׂיחִי אָנֹכִי
אֶשְׂמַח בַּיהוָה: יִתַּמּוּ
חַטָּאִים מִן־הָאָרֶץ וּרְשָׁעִים
עוֹד אֵינָם בָּרְכִי נַפְשִׁי אֶת־יְהוָה
הַלְלוּ־יָהּ:

Psalm 128

For individuals seeking livelihood, Psalm 128 is a source of encouragement and hope, promising that dedication to God's commandments leads to the enjoyment of the fruits of one's labor, prosperity, and a fulfilling family life.

A song of ascents. Happy are all who fear the Lord, who follow His ways. You shall enjoy the fruit of your labors; you shall be happy and you shall prosper. Your wife shall be like a fruitful vine within your house; your sons, like olive saplings around your table. So shall the man who fears the Lord be blessed. May the Lord bless you from Zion; may you share the prosperity of Jerusalem all the days of your life, and live to see your children's children. May all be well with Israel!

Shir hamma'alot ashrei kol-yerie adonai haholeich bidrachav. Yegia' kappecha ki tochel ashrecha vetov lach. Eshtecha kegefen poriyyah beyarketei veitecha banecha kishtilei zeitim saviv leshulchanecha. Hinneh chi-chen yevorach gaver yerei adonai. Yevarech'cha adonai mitziyyon ure'eih betuv yerushalaim kol yemei chayyeicha. Ure'eih-vanim levanecha shalom al-yisra'el.	שִׁיר הַמַּעֲלוֹת אַשְׁרֵי כָּל־יְרֵא יְהֹוָה הַהֹלֵךְ בִּדְרָכָיו: יְגִיעַ כַּפֶּיךָ כִּי תֹאכֵל אַשְׁרֶיךָ וְטוֹב לָךְ: אֶשְׁתְּךָ כְּגֶפֶן פֹּרִיָּה בְּיַרְכְּתֵי בֵיתֶךָ בָּנֶיךָ כִּשְׁתִלֵי זֵיתִים סָבִיב לְשֻׁלְחָנֶךָ: הִנֵּה כִי־כֵן יְבֹרַךְ גָּבֶר יְרֵא יְהֹוָה: יְבָרֶכְךָ יְהֹוָה מִצִּיּוֹן וּרְאֵה בְּטוּב יְרוּשָׁלָ͏ִם כֹּל יְמֵי חַיֶּיךָ: וּרְאֵה־בָנִים לְבָנֶיךָ שָׁלוֹם עַל־יִשְׂרָאֵל:

Psalm 145

Psalm 145 celebrates God's boundless generosity and meticulous care over creation. It highlights that all living beings depend on His grace for sustenance. For individuals striving for livelihood, these verses are a poignant reminder that God is the ultimate provider, attentively meeting the needs of every creature.

A song of praise. Of David. I will extol You, my God and king, and bless Your name forever and ever. Every day will I bless You and praise Your name forever and ever. Great is the Lord and much acclaimed; His greatness cannot be fathomed. One generation shall laud Your works to another and declare Your mighty acts. The glorious majesty of Your splendor and Your wondrous acts will I recite. Men shall talk of the might of Your awesome deeds, and I will recount Your greatness. They shall celebrate Your abundant goodness, and sing joyously of Your beneficence. The Lord is gracious and compassionate, slow to anger and abounding in kindness. The Lord is good to all, and His mercy is upon all His works. All Your works shall praise You, O Lord, and Your faithful ones shall bless You. They shall talk of the majesty of Your kingship, and speak of Your might, to make His mighty acts known among men and the majestic glory of His kingship. Your kingship is an eternal kingship; Your dominion is for all generations. The Lord supports all who stumble, and makes all who are bent stand straight. The eyes of all look to You expectantly, and You give them their food when it is due. You give it openhandedly, feeding every creature to its heart's content. The Lord is beneficent in all His ways and faithful in all His works. The Lord is near to all who call Him, to all who call Him with sincerity. He fulfills the wishes of those who fear Him; He hears their cry and delivers them. The Lord watches over all who love Him, but all the wicked He will destroy. My mouth shall utter the praise of the Lord, and all creatures shall bless His holy name forever and ever.

Tehillah ledavid aromimcha elohai
hammelech va'avarechah shimcha

תְּהִלָּה לְדָוִד אֲרוֹמִמְךָ אֱלוֹהַי
הַמֶּלֶךְ וַאֲבָרְכָה שְׁמֶךָ

le'olam va'ed. Bechol-yom
avarechekka va'ahallah shimcha
le'olam va'ed. Gadol adonai
umehullal me'od veligdullato ein
cheiker. Dor ledor yeshabbach
ma'asecha ugevurotecha
yaggidu. Hadar kevod hodecha
vedivrei nifle'otecha asichah.
Ve'ezuz nore'otecha yomeiru
ugedullatecha asapperennah.
Zeicher rav-tuvecha yabbi'u
vetzidkatecha yeranneinu.
Channun verachum adonai
erech appayim ugedal-
chased. Tov-adonai lakkol
verachamav al-kol-ma'asav.
Yoducha adonai kol-ma'asecha
vachasidecha yevarechuchah.
Kevod malchutecha yomeiru
ugevuratecha yedabbeiru.
Lehodia' livnei ha'adam gevurotav
uchevod hadar malchuto.
Malchutecha malchut kol-olamim
umemshaltecha bechol-dor vador.
Someich adonai lechol-hannofelim
vezokeif lechol-hakkefufim. Einei-
chol eleicha yesabbeiru ve'attah
notein-lahem et-ochlam be'itto.
Poteach et-yadecha umasbia'
lechol-chai ratzon. Tzaddik
adonai bechol-derachav vechasid
bechol-ma'asav. Karov adonai
lechol-kore'av lechol asher

לְעוֹלָם וָעֶד: בְּכָל־יוֹם
אֲבָרְכֶךָּ וַאֲהַלְלָה שִׁמְךָ
לְעוֹלָם וָעֶד: גָּדוֹל יְהוָה
וּמְהֻלָּל מְאֹד וְלִגְדֻלָּתוֹ אֵין
חֵקֶר: דּוֹר לְדוֹר יְשַׁבַּח
מַעֲשֶׂיךָ וּגְבוּרֹתֶיךָ
יַגִּידוּ: הֲדַר כְּבוֹד הוֹדֶךָ
וְדִבְרֵי נִפְלְאֹתֶיךָ אָשִׂיחָה:
וֶעֱזוּז נוֹרְאֹתֶיךָ יֹאמֵרוּ
וּגְדֻלָּתְךָ אֲסַפְּרֶנָּה:
זֵכֶר רַב־טוּבְךָ יַבִּיעוּ
וְצִדְקָתְךָ יְרַנֵּנוּ:
חַנּוּן וְרַחוּם יְהוָה
אֶרֶךְ אַפַּיִם וּגְדָל־
חָסֶד: טוֹב־יְהוָה לַכֹּל
וְרַחֲמָיו עַל־כָּל־מַעֲשָׂיו:
יוֹדוּךָ יְהוָה כָּל־מַעֲשֶׂיךָ
וַחֲסִידֶיךָ יְבָרְכוּכָה:
כְּבוֹד מַלְכוּתְךָ יֹאמֵרוּ
וּגְבוּרָתְךָ יְדַבֵּרוּ:
לְהוֹדִיעַ לִבְנֵי הָאָדָם גְּבוּרֹתָיו
וּכְבוֹד הֲדַר מַלְכוּתוֹ:
מַלְכוּתְךָ מַלְכוּת כָּל־עֹלָמִים
וּמֶמְשַׁלְתְּךָ בְּכָל־דּוֹר וָדֹר:
סוֹמֵךְ יְהוָה לְכָל־הַנֹּפְלִים
וְזוֹקֵף לְכָל־הַכְּפוּפִים:
עֵינֵי־כֹל אֵלֶיךָ יְשַׂבֵּרוּ
וְאַתָּה נוֹתֵן־לָהֶם אֶת־אָכְלָם
בְּעִתּוֹ: פּוֹתֵחַ אֶת־יָדֶךָ
וּמַשְׂבִּיעַ לְכָל־חַי רָצוֹן:
צַדִּיק יְהוָה בְּכָל־דְּרָכָיו
וְחָסִיד בְּכָל־מַעֲשָׂיו: קָרוֹב
יְהוָה לְכָל־קֹרְאָיו לְכֹל אֲשֶׁר

yikra'uhu ve'emet. Retzon-yere'av
ya'aseh ve'et-shav'atam yishma
veyoshi'eim. Shomer adonai et-
kol-ohavav ve'eit kol-haresha'im
yashmid. Tehillat adonai
yedabber-pi vivareich kol-basar
shem kodsho le'olam va'ed.

יִקְרָאֻהוּ בֶאֱמֶת: רְצוֹן־יְרֵאָיו
יַעֲשֶׂה וְאֶת־שַׁוְעָתָם יִשְׁמַע
וְיוֹשִׁיעֵם: שׁוֹמֵר יְהֹוָה אֶת־
כָּל־אֹהֲבָיו וְאֵת כָּל־הָרְשָׁעִים
יַשְׁמִיד: תְּהִלַּת יְהֹוָה
יְדַבֶּר־פִּי וִיבָרֵךְ כָּל־בָּשָׂר
שֵׁם קָדְשׁוֹ לְעוֹלָם וָעֶד:

Notes

_____
_____
_____
_____
_____
_____
_____
_____
_____
_____
_____
_____
_____
_____
_____
_____
_____

Prayers for Times of Difficulty

In times of difficulty, prayer provides strength, comfort, and guidance. The following prayers remind us that in our moments of struggle, we are not alone - our pleas and yearnings echo in the presence of the Divine, offering solace and support. As we navigate the challenges that life presents, these prayers encourage us to seek refuge and strength in our faith, affirming the ever-present help and protection that comes from turning towards God.

Prayer for Accepting Suffering with Love

I N HIS CLASSIC work, *Duties of the Hearts*, Rabbi Bechaya Ibn Pakuda (1050–1120) wrote that every challenge and pain that we experience is specially tailor-made for us by God. Though the pain is real, how we feel about it is up to us. By accepting what comes our way, we don't just get through the tough times, we grow from them.

The following is a prayer written by Rabbi Aharon Roth (1894-1947) about accepting our pain and suffering with love. It ends with a plea that all of our sins, the root of our suffering, be uprooted and that all suffering will be transformed into goodness and kindness.

I believe with complete faith that this pain and suffering that has come upon me is by the direct providence of the Lord, and I accept it lovingly. All this has come upon me because of my many sins, and You, O Lord, are righteous in all that has befallen me, for You have acted truthfully while I have acted wickedly. May it be Your will that these sufferings serve as atonement for my many sins. (And if it is an auspicious time, one may also say: And may this lighten the pain of our Mighty Sanctuary, so to speak, and the suffering of Israel). Indeed, according to justice, I would have needed to specify, repent, and confess for the sin and the transgression that caused these sufferings to come upon me. However, it is known and revealed before You that I do not know the extent. Therefore, may it be Your will, my Father in Heaven, that You erase, uproot, and remove the sin, transgression, and offense that have caused me these sufferings. May all harsh judgments be sweetened and lifted from me and from all of Israel. May all trials be transformed for good, and may good and revealed kindness be drawn to us and to all the House of Israel forever. Amen.

Ani ma'amin be'emunah sheleimah, shezzeh hatza'ar vehayyissurim shebba li hu behashgachah peratit mei'im adonai, vehin'ni mekabbeil alai be'ahavah, vechol zeh ba li mesibbot avonotai harabbim, ve'tzaddik attah adonai al kol habba alai ki emet asita va'ani hirsha'ti. Vihi ratzon sheyyihyu eillu hayyissurim lechapparah al avonotai harabbim (And if it is an auspicious time, one may also say: ulehakeil b'zeh tza'ar shechinnat uzeinu kivyachol vetza'aran shel yisra'el). Vehinneh mitzad haddin hayiti tzarich lefareit velashuv ulehitvaddot al hacheit veha'avon shebbesibbatam ba li eillu hayyissurim, aval galui veyadua' lefanecha she'ein itti yodea' ad mah. Lachein yehi ratzon millefanecha avi shebbashamayim, shettimchok uteshareish hacheit ve'avon ufesha sheggaremu li eillu hayyissurim, veyumteku kol haddinim mei'alai umei'al kol yisra'el, veyithappechu kol

אֲנִי מַאֲמִין בֶּאֱמוּנָה שְׁלֵמָה, שֶׁזֶּה הַצַּעַר וְהַיִּסּוּרִים שֶׁבָּא לִי הוּא בְּהַשְׁגָּחָה פְּרָטִית מֵעִם ה', וְהִנְנִי מְקַבֵּל עָלַי בְּאַהֲבָה, וְכָל זֶה בָּא לִי מִסִּבּוֹת עֲוֹנוֹתַי הָרַבִּים, וְצַדִּיק אַתָּה ה' עַל כָּל הַבָּא עָלַי כִּי אֱמֶת עָשִׂיתָ וַאֲנִי הִרְשַׁעְתִּי. וִיהִי רָצוֹן שֶׁיִּהְיוּ אֵלּוּ הַיִּסּוּרִים לְכַפָּרָה עַל עֲוֹנוֹתַי הָרַבִּים (ואם בעת רצון יאמר גם כן: וּלְהָקֵל בְּזֶה צַעַר שְׁכִנַּת עוּזֵינוּ כִּבְיָכוֹל וְצַעֲרָן שֶׁל יִשְׂרָאֵל). וְהִנֵּה מִצַּד הַדִּין הָיִיתִי צָרִיךְ לְפָרֵט וְלָשׁוּב וּלְהִתְוַדּוֹת עַל הַחֵטְא וְהֶעָוֹן שֶׁבְּסִבָּתָם בָּא לִי אֵלּוּ הַיִּסּוּרִים, אֲבָל גָּלוּי וְיָדוּעַ לְפָנֶיךָ שֶׁאֵין אִתִּי יוֹדֵעַ עַד מָה. לָכֵן יְהִי רָצוֹן מִלְּפָנֶיךָ אָבִי שֶׁבַּשָּׁמַיִם, שֶׁתִּמְחוֹק וּתְשָׁרֵשׁ הַחֵטְא וְעָוֹן וּפֶשַׁע שֶׁגָּרְמוּ לִי אֵלּוּ הַיִּסּוּרִים, וְיֻמְתְּקוּ כָּל הַדִּינִים מֵעָלַי וּמֵעַל כָּל יִשְׂרָאֵל, וְיִתְהַפְכוּ כָּל

hatzeirufim letovah, veyimshoch
chasadim tovim umegulim lanu
ulechol beit yisra'el ad olam.
Amein.

הַצֵרוּפִים לְטוֹבָה, וְיִמְשֹׁךְ
חֲסָדִים טוֹבִים וּמְגֻלִּים לָנוּ
וּלְכָל בֵּית יִשְׂרָאֵל עַד עוֹלָם.
אָמֵן.

Notes

Prayer for Divine Protection

THIS PRAYER, RECITED daily as part of the evening prayers, is a request for divine protection. It asks God to provide a life of peace and safety from all forms of harm by spreading His everlasting shelter upon us. Night is typically a time of unknown, of fear and vulnerability. It is at this time that we ask God to watch over us and protect us.

The Lord, our God; make us lie down in peace, our King, raise us again to life. Spread over us the shelter of Your peace, and direct us to better ourselves through Your good counsel; and deliver us for Your Name's sake. Shield us, and remove from us enemies, pestilence, sword, famine and sorrow. Remove the adversary from before us and from behind us, and shelter us in the shadow of Your wings. For, Almighty, You are our Protector and Rescuer, For, Almighty You are a gracious and merciful King. Guard our going out and our coming in for life and peace from now and forever. Blessed are You, Lord, Who guards His people Israel forever.

Hashkiveinu adonai eloheinu	הַשְׁכִּיבֵנוּ יְהֹוָה אֱלֹהֵינוּ
leshalom veha'amideinu malkeinu	לְשָׁלוֹם וְהַעֲמִידֵנוּ מַלְכֵּנוּ
lechayyim uferos aleinu sukkat	לְחַיִּים וּפְרוֹשׂ עָלֵינוּ סֻכַּת
shelomecha vetakkeneinu	שְׁלוֹמֶךָ וְתַקְּנֵנוּ
be'eitzah tovah millefanecha	בְּעֵצָה טוֹבָה מִלְּפָנֶיךָ
vehoshi'einu lema'an shemecha	וְהוֹשִׁיעֵנוּ לְמַעַן שְׁמֶךָ
vehagein ba'adeinu vehaser	וְהָגֵן בַּעֲדֵנוּ וְהָסֵר
mei'aleinu oyeiv dever vecherev	מֵעָלֵינוּ אוֹיֵב דֶּבֶר וְחֶרֶב
vera'av veyagon vehaseir satan	וְרָעָב וְיָגוֹן וְהָסֵר שָׂטָן
millefaneinu ume'achareinu	מִלְּפָנֵינוּ וּמֵאַחֲרֵינוּ
uvetzeil kenafecha tastireinu ki	וּבְצֵל כְּנָפֶיךָ תַּסְתִּירֵנוּ כִּי

eil shomereinu umatzileinu attah	אֵל שׁוֹמְרֵנוּ וּמַצִּילֵנוּ אָתָּה
ki eil melech channun verachum	כִּי אֵל מֶלֶךְ חַנּוּן וְרַחוּם
attah ushemor tzeteinu uvo'einu	אַתָּה וּשְׁמוֹר צֵאתֵנוּ וּבוֹאֵנוּ
lechayyim uleshalom mei'attah	לְחַיִּים וּלְשָׁלוֹם מֵעַתָּה
ve'ad olam: baruch attah adonai	וְעַד עוֹלָם: בָּרוּךְ אַתָּה יְהוָה
shomeir ammo yisra'el la'ad:	שׁוֹמֵר עַמּוֹ יִשְׂרָאֵל לָעַד:

Notes

_____

_____

_____

_____

_____

_____

_____

_____

_____

_____

_____

_____

_____

_____

_____

_____

_____

Prayer for a Safe Journey

The Traveler's Prayer, also referred to as the Wayfarer's Prayer or "Tefilat Haderech" in Hebrew, is traditionally recited at the beginning of a significant journey. It seeks divine protection for the traveler, asking for safe passage, safeguarding from potential hazards en route, and a peaceful return home.

May it be Your will, Eternal One, our God and the God of our ancestors, that You lead us toward peace, support our footsteps towards peace, guide us toward peace, and make us reach our desired destination, for life, joy, and peace. May You rescue us from the hand of every foe, ambush, bandits and wild animals along the way, and from all manner of punishments that assemble to come to Earth. May You send blessing in our every handiwork, and grant us peace, kindness, and mercy in your eyes and in the eyes of all who see us. May You hear the sound of our supplication, because You are the God who hears prayer and supplications. Blessed are You, Eternal One, who hears prayer.

Yehi ratzon milfanecha adonai	יְהִי רָצוֹן מִלְפָנֶיךָ יי
eloheinu veilohei avoteinu,	אֱלֹהֵינוּ וֵאלֹהֵי אֲבוֹתֵינוּ,
shettolicheinu leshalom	שֶׁתּוֹלִיכֵנוּ לְשָׁלוֹם
vetatz'ideinu leshalom	וְתַצְעִידֵנוּ לְשָׁלוֹם
vetadricheinu leshalom,	וְתַדְרִיכֵנוּ לְשָׁלוֹם,
vetismecheinu leshalom,	וְתִסְמְכֵנוּ לְשָׁלוֹם,
vetaggi'einu limchoz cheftzeinu	וְתַגִּיעֵנוּ לִמְחוֹז חֶפְצֵנוּ
lechayyim ulesimchah uleshalom.	לְחַיִּים וּלְשִׂמְחָה וּלְשָׁלוֹם.
Vetatzileinu mikkaf kol oyeiv	וְתַצִּילֵנוּ מִכַּף כָּל אוֹיֵב
ve'oreiv velistim vechayyot	וְאוֹרֵב וְלִסְטִים וְחַיּוֹת

ra'ot badderech, umikkol minei
pur'anuyyot hammittraggeshot
lavo la'olam, vetitteneinu
lechein ulechesed ulerachamim
be'einecha uv'einei chol ro'einu,
ki eil shomei'a tefillah vetachanun
attah. Baruch attah adonai
shomei'a tefillah:

רָעוֹת בַּדֶּרֶךְ, וּמִכָּל מִינֵי
פֻּרְעָנִיּוֹת הַמִּתְרַגְּשׁוֹת
לָבוֹא לָעוֹלָם, וְתִתְּנֵנוּ
לְחֵן וּלְחֶסֶד וּלְרַחֲמִים
בְּעֵינֶיךָ וּבְעֵינֵי כָל רֹאֵינוּ,
כִּי אֵל שׁוֹמֵעַ תְּפִלָּה וְתַחֲנוּן
אַתָּה. בָּרוּךְ אַתָּה יְיָ
שׁוֹמֵעַ תְּפִלָּה:

Notes

_____

_____

_____

_____

_____

_____

_____

_____

_____

_____

_____

_____

_____

_____

Prayer to Overcome Fear

T HE FOLLOWING SHORT prayer, found at the end of the daily service, is a combination of Proverbs 3:25, Isaiah 8:10 and Isaiah 46:4. It offers a powerful reassurance against fear and adversity, reminding us of the divine promise of protection and support.

Do not fear sudden terror nor the destruction of the wicked when it comes. Plan a conspiracy together but it will be foiled; speak your piece and it will not stand, for God is with us. To your old age I am with you, and even till your ripe old age, I shall endure. I have made you, and I will bear you; I shall endure and rescue.

Al tira mippachad pitom umisho'at resha'im ki tavo utzu eitzah vetufar dabberu davar velo yakum ki immanu el: ve'ad ziknah ani hu ve'ad seivah ani esbol: ani asiti va'ani esa va'ani esbol va'amalleit:

אַל תִּירָא מִפַּחַד פִּתְאֹם וּמִשֹּׁאַת
רְשָׁעִים כִּי תָבֹא עֻצוּ עֵצָה וְתֻפָר
דַּבְּרוּ דָבָר וְלֹא יָקוּם כִּי
עִמָּנוּ אֵל: וְעַד זִקְנָה אֲנִי הוּא
וְעַד שֵׂיבָה אֲנִי אֶסְבֹּל: אֲנִי עָשִׂיתִי
וַאֲנִי אֶשָּׂא וַאֲנִי אֶסְבֹּל וַאֲמַלֵּט:

Notes

_____

_____

_____

_____

_____

Prisoner's Prayer

T HE FOLLOWING IS a prayer for release from captivity written by Rabbi Chaim Palagi (1788-1868). Drawing inspiration from the story of Noah, this prayer is a fervent request of God to be freed from confinement and to be led into a life of peace and goodness.

Master of all worlds, take me out of this confinement to a good life and peace, for my soul is weary from being closed in. May all the righteous crown You with a crown of kingship for taking me out of this confinement, as it is said: "You have brought out my soul from confinement to give thanks to Your name; the righteous shall crown You for You have dealt bountifully with me."

And just as You accepted Noah's prayer when he was closed in the ark and You brought him, his wife, his sons, his sons' wives, and all that was theirs out, so too, answer me and bring us out of this confinement to a good life and peace, to give thanks to Your name always, all the days. Amen, may it be Your will.

Ribbon kol ha'olamim hotzi'ani	רִבּוֹן כָּל הָעוֹלָמִים הוֹצִיאֵנִי
min hammasger hazzeh lechayyim	מִן הַמַּסְגֵּר הַזֶּה לְחַיִּים
tovim uleshalom ki ayeifah nafshi	טוֹבִים וּלְשָׁלוֹם כִּי עֲיֵפָה נַפְשִׁי
mihyot sagur veyachtiru lecha	מִהְיוֹת סָגוּר וְיַכְתִּירוּ לְךָ
kol hatzaddikim keter malchut	כָּל הַצַּדִּיקִים כֶּתֶר מַלְכוּת
shehotzeitani min hammasger	שֶׁהוֹצֵאתַנִי מִן הַמַּסְגֵּר
hazzeh shenne'emar hotzi'ah	הַזֶּה שֶׁנֶּאֱמַר הוֹצִיאָה
mimmasger nafshi lehodot et	מִמַּסְגֵּר נַפְשִׁי לְהוֹדוֹת אֶת
shemecha bi yachtiru tzaddikim ki	שְׁמֶךָ בִּי יַכְתִּרוּ צַדִּיקִים כִּי
tigmol alai.	תִגְמֹל עָלָי.

Uchesheim shekkibbalta tefillat
noach keshehayah sagur
batteivah vehotzeita lo ule'ishto
ulevanav uneshei banav vechol
asher lahem, kach te'anneini
vetotzi'einnu min hammasgeir
hazzeh le'chayyim tovim
uleshalom lehodot et shimcha
tamid kol hayyamim. Amen kein
yehi ratzon.

וּכְשֵׁם שֶׁקִּבַּלְתָּ תְּפִלַּת
נֹחַ כְּשֶׁהָיָה סָגוּר
בַּתֵּבָה וְהוֹצֵאתָ לוֹ וּלְאִשְׁתּוֹ
וּלְבָנָיו וּנְשֵׁי בָנָיו וְכָל
אֲשֶׁר לָהֶם כָּךְ תַּעֲנֵנִי
וְתוֹצִיאֵנוּ מִן הַמַּסְגֵּר
הַזֶּה לְחַיִּים טוֹבִים
וּלְשָׁלוֹם לְהוֹדוֹת אֶת שִׁמְךָ
תָּמִיד כָּל הַיָּמִים אָמֵן כֵּן
יְהִי רָצוֹן.

Notes

_____

_____

_____

_____

_____

_____

_____

_____

_____

_____

_____

_____

_____

Prayer for Women Suffering From Domestic Violence

CRAFTED BY DR. Yael Levine for the International Day for the Elimination of Violence Against Women, this prayer appeals to God for mercy on the women who suffer abuse from their partners. It calls for divine intervention to heal, protect, and uplift these women, fostering peace and dignity in their lives. It's a poignant plea against domestic violence, seeking a world in which all women are cherished and respected.

May it be Your will, Lord our God and God of our ancestors, God of Abraham, Isaac, and Jacob, Sarah, Rebecca, Rachel, and Leah, that You bestow mercy on all the women whose partners are violent towards them, who strike them, harm them, oppress and disgrace them; their lives are not lives. See the affliction and pain of the women suffering from their partners, for a woman enters matrimony to have a good existence, not to suffer pain. May Your mercy be stirred for the women whose partners instill terror and dread in them.

Incline Your ear, O God, and hear; open Your eyes and listen to the cries of the women suffering under the hands of their partners. Their tears are frequent, and may it be Your will, You Who hears the voice of weeping, that You place their tears in Your flask to be kept. Do not hide Your face from them, and extend Your right hand to draw them close, support them, and protect them as the apple of Your eye. Send Your help from the sanctuary, and open their hearts so that others will help them.

And bring them out of their distress, redeem them from their anguish, and may it be fulfilled in them the verse that is written: "When I call upon you, answer me, O God of my righteousness; in (previous) distress You have relieved me; have now mercy on me and hear my prayer" (Psalms 4:2). And break the pride and power of the men who dare to raise a hand against their partners.

Raise the dignity of the women stifled under the yoke of their partners, grant cure and healing to all their pains, and bestow upon them blessing and peace. Decree upon them good decrees, salvations, and consolations, fulfill their wishes for good, and establish peace between man and his wife, and let us say, Amen.

Yehi ratzon millefanecha adonai	יְהִי רָצוֹן מִלְפָנֶיךָ ה׳
e-loheinu vei-lohei avoteinu,	אֱ-לֹהֵינוּ וֵא-לֹהֵי אֲבוֹתֵינוּ,
e-lohei avraham yitzchak	אֱ-לֹהֵי אַבְרָהָם יִצְחָק
veya'akov sarah rivkah rachel	וְיַעֲקֹב שָׂרָה רִבְקָה רָחֵל
vele'ah, shettitmallei rachamim	וְלֵאָה, שֶׁתִּתְמַלֵּא רַחֲמִים
al kol hannashim asher benei	עַל כָּל הַנָּשִׁים אֲשֶׁר בְּנֵי
zugan allimim heim, umakkim otan	זוּגָן אַלִּימִים הֵם, וּמַכִּים אוֹתָן
vechovlim bahen, umetza'arim	וְחוֹבְלִים בָּהֶן, וּמְצַעֲרִים
umevazzim otan, vechayyeihen	וּמְבַזִּים אוֹתָן, וְחַיֵּיהֶן
einam chayyim. Re'eih et onyan	אֵינָם חַיִּים. רְאֵה אֶת עָנְיָן
umach'ovan shel hannashim	וּמַכְאוֹבָן שֶׁל הַנָּשִׁים
hasheruyot betza'ar uvetzarah	הַשְּׁרוּיוֹת בְּצַעַר וּבְצָרָה
mechamat benei zugan,	מֵחֲמַת בְּנֵי זוּגָן,
sheha'ishah lechayyim nittnah	שֶׁהָאִשָּׁה לְחַיִּים נִתְּנָה
velo letza'ar. Veyikkamru	וְלֹא לְצַעַר. וְיִכָּמְרוּ
rachamecha al hannashim	רַחֲמֶיךָ עַל הַנָּשִׁים
shebbenei zugan metilim aleihen	שֶׁבְּנֵי זוּגָן מְטִילִים עֲלֵיהֶן
eimatah vafachad.	אֵימָתָה וָפַחַד.
Hatteih e-lohai oznecha ushema,	הַטֵּה אֱ-לֹהַי אָזְנְךָ וּשְׁמַע,

פְּקַח עֵינֶיךָ, וְהַקְשִׁיבָה
לְקוֹל שַׁוְעַת הַנָּשִׁים
הַמִּתְעַנּוֹת תַּחַת יְדֵי
בְּנֵי זוּגָן. הָאִשָּׁה דִּמְעָתָהּ
מְצוּיָה, וִיהִי רָצוֹן מִלְּפָנֶיךָ
שׁוֹמֵעַ קוֹל בְּכִיּוֹת שֶׁתָּשִׂים
דִּמְעוֹתֵיהֶן שֶׁל נָשִׁים אֵלֶּה
בְּנֹאדְךָ לִהְיוֹת. אַל תַּסְתֵּר
פָּנֶיךָ מֵהֶן, וִימִינְךָ תְּהֵא
פְּשׁוּטָה לְקָרְבָן וּלְסַעֲדָן
וּלְשָׁמְרָן כְּאִישׁוֹן בַּת עָיִן.
וּשְׁלַח עֶזְרְךָ מִקֹּדֶשׁ,
וּפְתַח אֶת לִבָּן וְיֵאֹתוּ
שֶׁהַבְּרִיּוֹת יַעַזְרוּ לָהֶן.

pekach einecha, vehakshiva
lekol shav'at hannashim
hammit'annot tachat yedei
benei zugan. Ha'ishah dimata
metzuyah, vihi ratzon millefanecha
shomei'a kol bichyot shettasim
dimoteihen shel nashim eilleh
benodcha lihyot. Al tasteir
panecha meihen, vimincha tehei
peshutah lekorvan ulesa'adan
uleshomran ke'ishon bat ayin.
Ushelach ezrecha mikkodesh,
ufetach et libban veyei'otu
shehabberiyyot ya'azru lahen.

וְהוֹצִיאֵן מִמְּצֻקוֹתֵיהֶן
וּפְדֵה אוֹתָן מִצָּרָתָן, וִיקֻיַּם
בָּהֶן מִקְרָא שֶׁכָּתוּב: "בְּקָרְאִי
עֲנֵנִי אֱ-לֹהֵי צִדְקִי, בַּצָּר
הִרְחַבְתָּ לִּי, חָנֵּנִי וּשְׁמַע
תְּפִלָּתִי" (תהילים ד, ב). וּשְׁבֹר אֶת
גְּאוֹן עֻזָּם שֶׁל הַגְּבָרִים
הַמַּרְהִיבִים לְהָרִים יָד עַל בְּנוֹת
זוּגָם.

Vehotzi'ein mimmetzukoteihen
ufedeih otan mitzaratan, vikuyyam
bahen mikra shekkatuv: "Bekorii
aneini e-lohei tzidki, batzar
hirchavta li, chonneini ushema
tefillati" (Psalms 4:2). Ushevor et
ge'on uzzam shel haggevarim
hammarhivim leharim yad al benot
zugam.

הָרֵם אֶת קַרְנָן שֶׁל הַנָּשִׁים
הַנֶּאֱנָקוֹת תַּחַת עוֹל בְּנֵי
זוּגָן, וְהַעֲלֵה אֲרוּכָה
וּמַרְפֵּא לְכָל מַכְאוֹבֵיהֶן,
וְהָבֵא עֲלֵיהֶן בְּרָכָה
וְשָׁלוֹם, וּגְזֹר עֲלֵיהֶן גְּזֵרוֹת
טוֹבוֹת יְשׁוּעוֹת וְנֶחָמוֹת,
וּמַלֵּא מִשְׁאֲלוֹתֵיהֶן לְטוֹבָה,

Hareim et karnan shel hannashim
hanne'enakot tachat ol benei
zugan, veha'aleih aruchah
umarpei lechol mach'oveihen,
vehavei aleihen berachah
veshalom, ugezor aleihen gezeirot
tovot yeshu'ot venechamot,
umallei mish'aloteihen letovah,

vesim shalom bein ish le'ishto,
venomar amen.

וְשִׂים שָׁלוֹם בֵּין אִישׁ לְאִשְׁתּוֹ,
וְנֹאמַר אָמֵן.

Notes

_____

_____

_____

_____

_____

_____

_____

_____

_____

_____

_____

_____

_____

_____

_____

_____

_____

_____

_____

_____

Prayer Following a Divorce
תְּפִלָּה לָאִשָּׁה לְאַחַר קַבָּלַת הַגֵּט

I N THE AFTERMATH of a dissolved marriage, this prayer, written by Dr. Yael Levine, is a poignant expression of hope and healing, seeking direction and peace from the Creator. It is a sincere request for tranquility, guidance, and a future blessed with love and companionship.

The marriage covenant we made has been broken and has come to an end. My gaze is now turned forward to the future.

I cast my supplication before You, Creator of heaven and earth, that I may find tranquility for my soul, calmness and confidence for my spirit, and peace and serenity in my heart.

Please bestow upon me an abundance of blessings from the source of all blessings, guide my path at this time, and turn my fortune from now for the better.

Merit and assist me to find a suitable partner, and may we enter into a marriage of eternal love, a holy covenant, and a covenant of peace.

"God, hear my prayer, listen to the words of my mouth" (Psalms 54:4).

Berit hannissu'in shekkaratnu
hufrah vehiggi'ah lidei siyyum.
Mabbati mufneh attah kadimah el
eiver he'atid.

בְּרִית הַנִּשּׂוּאִין שֶׁכָּרַתְנוּ
הוּפְרָה וְהִגִּיעָה לִידֵי סִיּוּם.
מַבָּטִי מֻפְנֶה עַתָּה קָדִימָה אֶל
עֵבֶר הֶעָתִיד.

Ani mappilah et techinnati lefanecha, borei shamayim va'aretz, ki emtza margo'a lenafshi, hashkeit vavetach lenishmati, veshalom veshalvah bilvavi.

אֲנִי מַפִּילָה אֶת תְּחִנָּתִי לְפָנֶיךָ, בּוֹרֵא שָׁמַיִם וָאָרֶץ, כִּי אֶמְצָא מַרְגּוֹעַ לְנַפְשִׁי, הַשְׁקֵט וָבֶטַח לְנִשְׁמָתִי, וְשָׁלוֹם וְשַׁלְוָה בִּלְבָבִי.

Na hashpa alai shefa berachot mimmekor habberachot, hatzlach et darki ba'eit hazzot, vahafoch et mazzali mei'attah letov.

נָא הַשְׁפַּע עָלַי שֶׁפַע בְּרָכוֹת מִמְּקוֹר הַבְּרָכוֹת, הַצְלַח אֶת דַּרְכִּי בָּעֵת הַזֹּאת, וַהֲכֹךְ אֶת מַזָּלִי מֵעַתָּה לְטוֹב.

Zakkeini ve'ozreini limtzo et ben zugi hara'ui li, ve'avo immo bekishrei kelulot; be'ahavat olam, bivrit kodesh uvivrit shalom.

זַכֵּנִי וְעָזְרֵנִי לִמְצֹא אֶת בֶּן זוּגִי הָרָאוּי לִי, וְאָבוֹא עִמּוֹ בְּקִשְׁרֵי כְּלוּלוֹת; בְּאַהֲבַת עוֹלָם, בִּבְרִית קֹדֶשׁ וּבִבְרִית שָׁלוֹם.

E-lohim shema tefillati ha'azinah le'imrei fi (Psalms 54:4).

אֱ-לֹהִים שְׁמַע תְּכִלָּתִי הַאֲזִינָה לְאִמְרֵי פִי (תהילים נד, ד).

Notes

_____

_____

_____

_____

_____

_____

_____

Prayer for Wellbeing in Old Age

THIS PRAYER BY Rabbi Chaim Palagi (1788-1868) is a profound appeal to God expressing a desire for strength, health, and spiritual integrity throughout old age and until the end of life. It seeks God's mercy for the preservation of physical and mental faculties, the well-being of future generations, and protection against all harm, even as one grows old.

Master of all worlds and Lord of Lords, I Am that I Am, do not weaken my hand in my old age from engaging in study of the Bible and from fulfilling the commandments. Do not cast me aside in old age; when my strength fails, do not forsake me, and do not let my teeth weaken with my sons and daughters, my grandsons and granddaughters, that none of them shall die in my lifetime. May I always be settled in my mind and my intellect to serve You truthfully, and let there be no blemish in my offspring until the end of all generations. Give me strength, health, courage, and fortitude in all my limbs and sinews. May Your mercies please be stirred upon me to give strength in all my limbs so that they do not falter or weaken. May my sleep be sweet on my bed, and save me from all evil spirits, and may I have a good old age, that my eyes do not dim, and my legs do not falter, and my limbs do not weaken. Renew my youth like the eagle's, heal me and revive me, and let not my sustenance be interrupted, and let me not lose my freshness, until after a long life, in a death of kissing may "I come to the grave at a ripe old age, as the grain stack is taken away in its time," a full life. Heal me, O Lord, and I will be healed; save me, and I will be saved, for You are my praise, for You hear the prayer of every mouth. Blessed are You who hears prayer, Amen.

Ribbon ha'olamim va'adonei
ha'adonim, ehyeh asher ehyeh,
al tarpeh et yadi le'eit ziknati
milla'asok battorah umillekayyem
hammitzvot, al tashlicheini le'eit
ziknah, kichlot kochi al ta'azveini,
ve'al takheh et shinnai bevanai
uvivnotai venechdi venechdotai,
shello yamutu shum echad
mehem bechayyai, vetamid
ehyeh meyushevet beda'ti
vesichli le'avdecha be'emet,
velo yihyeh pasul bezar'i ad sof
kol haddorot, vetein bi koach
uveri'ut ve'ometz vechozek
bechol eivarai vegidai, veyehemu
na rachamecha alai lateit bi
koach bechol eivarai shello
yazuvu velo yid'avu, ute'areiv
shenati al mishkavi vetatzileini
mikkol ruchot ra'ot veyihyeh
li seivah tovah, shello yakhu
einai velo yim'adu karsullai, velo
yachloshu eivarai, utechaddeish
kenesher ne'urai, vetachlimeini
utechayyeini velo yitbattelu
mezonotai, velo yanus lachai, ad
achar arichut yamim veshanim
bemittat neshikah kechelach alai
kaver, ka'alot gadish be'itto seva
yamim. Refei'ani adonai ve'eirafei,
hoshi'eini ve'ivvashei'ah ki tehillati
attah, ki attah shomei'a tefillat

רִבּוֹן הָעוֹלָמִים וַאֲדוֹנֵי
הָאֲדוֹנִים, אֶהְיֶה אֲשֶׁר אֶהְיֶה,
אַל תַּרְפֶּה אֶת יָדִי לְעֵת זִקְנָתִי
מִלַּעֲסֹק בַּתּוֹרָה וּמִלְּקַיֵּם
הַמִּצְוֹת, אַל תַּשְׁלִיכֵנִי לְעֵת
זִקְנָה, כִּכְלוֹת כֹּחִי אַל תַּעַזְבֵנִי,
וְאַל תַּקְהֶה אֶת שִׁנַּי בְּבָנַי
וּבִכְנוֹתַי וְנֶכְדִּי וְנֶכְדּוֹתַי,
שֶׁלֹּא יָמוּתוּ שׁוּם אֶחָד
מֵהֶם בְּחַיַּי, וְתָמִיד
אֶהְיֶה מְיֻשֶּׁבֶת בְּדַעְתִּי
וְשִׂכְלִי לְעָבְדְּךָ בֶּאֱמֶת,
וְלֹא יִהְיֶה פָּסוּל בְּזַרְעִי עַד סוֹף
כָּל הַדּוֹרוֹת, וְתֶן בִּי כֹּחַ
וּבְרִיאוּת וְאֹמֶץ וְחֹזֶק
בְּכָל אֵבָרַי וְגִידַי, וְיֶהֱמוּ
נָא רַחֲמֶיךָ עָלַי לָתֵת בִּי
כֹּחַ בְּכָל אֵבָרַי שֶׁלֹּא
יָזוּבוּ וְלֹא יִדְאֲבוּ, וּתְעָרֵב
שְׁנָתִי עַל מִשְׁכָּבִי וְתַצִּילֵנִי
מִכָּל רוּחוֹת רָעוֹת וְיִהְיֶה
לִי שֵׂיבָה טוֹבָה, שֶׁלֹּא יָקְהוּ
עֵינַי וְלֹא יִמְעֲדוּ קַרְסֻלַּי, וְלֹא
יַחְלְשׁוּ אֵבָרַי, וּתְחַדֵּשׁ
כַּנֶּשֶׁר נְעוּרַי, וְתַחְלִימֵנִי
וּתְחַיֵּנִי וְלֹא יִתְבַּטְּלוּ
מְזוֹנוֹתַי, וְלֹא יָנוּס לֵחַי, עַד
אַחַר אֲרִיכוּת יָמִים וְשָׁנִים
בְּמִתַת נְשִׁיקָה כְּ"כָלַח אֱלֵי־
קָבֶר, כַּעֲלוֹת גָּדִישׁ בְּעִתּוֹ" שֶׁבַע
יָמִים. רְפָאֵנִי ה' וְאֵרָפֵא,
הוֹשִׁיעֵנִי וְאִוָּשֵׁעָה כִּי תְהִלָּתִי
אָתָּה, כִּי אַתָּה שׁוֹמֵעַ תְּפִלַּת

kol peh, baruch shomei'a tefillah, amen

כָּל פֶּה, בָּרוּךְ שׁוֹמֵעַ תְּפִלָּה,
אָמֵן

Notes

_____
_____
_____
_____
_____
_____
_____
_____
_____
_____
_____
_____
_____
_____
_____
_____
_____
_____
_____
_____
_____
_____

Prayers for Family

The prayers in this section reflect on our most important relationships, asking for divine guidance and blessings for their success. Rooted in deep faith, they express the earnest desires for companionship, the blessing of children, family harmony and well-being. They underscore the power of prayer and divine grace in establishing and enriching these relationships.

Prayer for a Soulmate

T HE FOLLOWING PRAYER, composed by Rabbi Isaiah Horowitz (1570-1626), a distinguished rabbi of the late 16th and early 17th centuries, is a heartfelt plea for finding a soulmate. It expresses a deep desire for a partner who will complement the person praying, help them grow, and who shares the aspiration for a life filled with goodness, generosity, and kindness.

May it be Your will Hashem, my God and God of my forefathers, that You find for me with Your many mercies and the greatness of Your kindness, my true and befitting marriage partner at the right time. The right partner, worthy of having children, a learned man, great in knowledge of the Bible and the fear of Heaven, born from the seed of righteous and truthful men who have fear of sin. Just like You found the true partner for Adam, the first man, for Abraham, Isaac, Jacob and Moses, each one his true partner at the right moment and time. And please let the partner that You choose for me be a good man, one with pleasantness of action, a master of good deeds, a man of grace with intelligence and fear of God, a pursuer of charity and a doer of kindnesses.

May he not have even a little insufficiency, or physical defect, or imperfection, and not be an angry or aggressive man. May he just be modest with a humble spirit, healthy, and strong. And please don't allow any interference from ruthless individuals or enemies whose intentions and manipulations would aspire to prevent me from meeting my marriage partner.

May the words of my mouth and the thoughts of my heart find favor before You, Hashem, my Rock and my Redeemer.

Yehi ratzon millefaneicha, adonai elohai veilohei avotai, shettamtzi li berachamecha harabbim uvachasadecha haggedolim et zivugi hara'ui li bizmanno. Zivug hagun hara'ui leholid talmid chacham, gadol b'torah uvyir'ah, mizzera tzaddikim ve'anshei emet vir'ei cheit, kemo shehimtzeita zivugo shel adam harishon, le'avraham veyitzchak veya'akov umosheh, kol echad ve'echad zivugo be'itto uvizmanno. Ve'oto ish shettamtzi li lezivugi yehe: ish tov, ish na'eh bema'asav vena'eh bemar'eihu, ba'al ma'asim tovim, ba'al chein, ish maskil virei elohim, rodeif tzedakah vegomeil chesed.

Velo yehei bo shum shemetz pesul umum ufegam. Velo yehei ka'asan veragzan, rak yehei ba'al anavah unemichut ruach, bari uva'al koach. Ve'al ye'akkeiv achzariyyut habberiyyot vesone'im umachshevoteihem vetachbuloteihem umo'atzoteihem, le'akkeiv et ben zugi hahuchan li. Vikuyyam bi mikra shekkatuv, lo yanuach shevet haresha al goral hatzaddikim, umikra shekkatuv, eshtecha kegefen

יְהִי רָצוֹן מִלְּפָנֶיךָ, יְיָ אֱלֹהַי וֵאלֹהֵי אֲבוֹתַי, שֶׁתַּמְצִיא לִי בְּרַחֲמֶיךָ הָרַבִּים וּבַחֲסָדֶיךָ הַגְּדוֹלִים אֶת זִוּוּגִי הָרָאוּי לִי בִּזְמַנּוֹ. זִוּוּג הָגוּן הָרָאוּי לְהוֹלִיד תַּלְמִיד חָכָם, גָּדוֹל בְּתוֹרָה וּבְיִרְאָה, מִזֶּרַע צַדִּיקִים וְאַנְשֵׁי אֱמֶת וְיִרְאֵי חֵטְא, כְּמוֹ שֶׁהִמְצֵאתָ זִוּוּגוֹ שֶׁל אָדָם הָרִאשׁוֹן, לְאַבְרָהָם וְיִצְחָק וְיַעֲקֹב וּמֹשֶׁה, כָּל אֶחָד וְאֶחָד זִוּוּגוֹ בְּעִתּוֹ וּבִזְמַנּוֹ. וְאוֹתוֹ אִישׁ שֶׁתַּמְצִיא לִי לְזִוּוּגִי יְהֵא: אִישׁ טוֹב, אִישׁ נָאֶה בְּמַעֲשָׂיו וְנָאֶה בְּמַרְאֵהוּ, בַּעַל מַעֲשִׂים טוֹבִים, בַּעַל חֵן, אִישׁ מַשְׂכִּיל וִירֵא אֱלֹהִים, רוֹדֵף צְדָקָה וְגוֹמֵל חֶסֶד.

וְלֹא יְהֵא בּוֹ שׁוּם שֶׁמֶץ פְּסוּל וּמוּם וּפְגָם. וְלֹא יְהֵא כַּעֲסָן וְרַגְזָן, רַק יְהֵא בַּעַל עֲנָוָה וּנְמִיכוּת רוּחַ, בָּרִיא וּבַעַל כֹּחַ. וְאַל יְעַכֵּב אַכְזָרִיּוּת הַבְּרִיּוֹת וְשׂוֹנְאִים וּמַחְשְׁבוֹתֵיהֶם וְתַחְבּוּלוֹתֵיהֶם וּמוֹעֲצוֹתֵיהֶם, לְעַכֵּב אֶת בֶּן זִוּוּגִי הַהוּכָן לִי. וִיקֻיַּם בִּי מִקְרָא שֶׁכָּתוּב, לֹא יָנוּחַ שֵׁבֶט הָרֶשַׁע עַל גּוֹרַל הַצַּדִּיקִים, וּמִקְרָא שֶׁכָּתוּב, אֶשְׁתְּךָ כְּגֶפֶן

poriyyah beyarketei beitecha,
banecha kishtilei zeitim saviv
leshulchanecha. Ki attah hu
hammoshiv yechidim bayyetah
motzi asirim bakkosharot.

Yihyu leratzon imrei fi vehegyon
libbi lefanecha, adonai tzuri
vego'ali.

פֹּרִיָּה בְּיַרְכְּתֵי בֵיתֶךָ,
בָּנֶיךָ כִּשְׁתִלֵי זֵיתִים סָבִיב
לְשֻׁלְחָנֶךָ. כִּי אַתָּה הוּא
הַמּוֹשִׁיב יְחִידִים בַּיְתָה
מוֹצִיא אֲסִירִים בַּכּוֹשָׁרוֹת.

יִהְיוּ לְרָצוֹן אִמְרֵי פִי וְהֶגְיוֹן
לִבִּי לְפָנֶיךָ, יְיָ צוּרִי
וְגוֹאֲלִי.

Notes

Prayer for a Successful Marriage

T HIS PRAYER IS a request for harmony, love, peace and friendship within one's marriage.

May it be Your will before You, Lord our God and God of our ancestors, Lord of peace, King to whom peace belongs, that love and brotherhood, peace and friendship, reign between me (say your name and your mother's name) and my husband (say his name and his mother's name) from now and forever. Save us quickly for Your name's sake and protect us, and deliver us from every evil person, from all trouble and harm, and nullify the plans of anyone who devises evil against us and against Your people, the house of Israel, any counsel that is not good and any harmful thought, as it is written, "Devise your strategy, but it will be thwarted; propose your plan, but it will not stand, for God is with us." And remove from us all conflict, jealousy, hatred, and competition, and for Your name's sake, God Almighty, remove from us all adversaries and accusers, whether above or below, and let them have no power to harm or accuse us. And command Your angels to help and assist us, as it is written, "No harm will overtake you, no disaster will come near your tent. For He will command His angels concerning you to guard you in all your ways."

Please, Lord, compassionate and gracious God, slow to anger, abounding in kindness and truth, creator of light and creator of darkness, maker of peace and creator of everything, let not our sins prevent the good from us, and incline our hearts to honor one another, and let Your Presence dwell among us, and let there be among us love and brotherhood, peace and friendship, light and joy from now and forever. And fulfill in us the verse, "He will make your borders peaceful and satisfy you with the finest wheat." And fulfill in my husband the verse, "May there be peace within your walls and security within your citadels." And bless me with the blessing written in Your Torah: "The Lord bless you and keep you; the Lord make His face shine on you and be gracious to you; the Lord lift up His countenance on you and give you peace," and fill us with great mercy and fulfill all the desires of our heart for good and for blessing, and fulfill in my husband the verse, "The Spirit of the Lord will rest on him— the Spirit of wisdom and of understanding, the Spirit of counsel and of might, the Spirit of knowledge and of the fear of the Lord," Amen, may it be Your will forever, Selah and forever.

The Lord will give strength to His people; the Lord will bless His people with peace. May the words of my mouth and the meditation of my heart be pleasing in your sight, Lord, my Rock and my Redeemer.

The Lord Almighty is with us; the God of Jacob is our fortress, Selah. Happy is the man who trusts in You. Lord, save us; may the King answer us when we call.

Yehi ratzon millefanecha adonai	יְהִי רָצוֹן מִלְּפָנֶיךָ יְיָ
eloheinu veilohei avvteinu adon	אֱלֹהֵינוּ וֵאלֹהֵי אֲבוֹתֵינוּ אֲדוֹן
hashalom melech shehashalom	הַשָּׁלוֹם מֶלֶךְ שֶׁהַשָּׁלוֹם
shello, shettashreh ahavah	שֶׁלּוֹ, שֶׁתַּשְׁרֶה אַהֲבָה
ve'achavah, shalom verei'ut beini	וְאַחֲוָה, שָׁלוֹם וְרֵעוּת בֵּינִי (וְתֹאמַר
(wife's name)	אֶת שְׁמָהּ וְשֵׁם אִמָּהּ: פְּלוֹנִית בַּת
levein ba'ali	פְּלוֹנִית) לְבֵין בַּעֲלִי (וְתֹאמַר אֶת
(husband's name)	שְׁמוֹ וְשֵׁם אִמּוֹ: פְּלוֹנִי בֶּן פְּלוֹנִית)
mei'attah ve'ad olam vehoshi'einu	מֵעַתָּה וְעַד עוֹלָם וְהוֹשִׁיעֵנוּ
meheirah lema'an shemecha	מְהֵרָה לְמַעַן שְׁמֶךָ
vehaggen ba'adeinu vetatzileinu	וְהָגֵן בַּעֲדֵנוּ וְתַצִּילֵנוּ

mikkol adam ra umikkol tzar	מִכָּל אָדָם רַע וּמִכָּל צַר
umazzik, vechol hayyo'etz aleinu	וּמַזִּיק, וְכָל הַיּוֹעֵץ עָלֵינוּ
ve'al ammecha beit yisra'el eitzah	וְעַל עַמְּךָ בֵּית יִשְׂרָאֵל עֵצָה
she'einah tovah umachshavah	שֶׁאֵינָה טוֹבָה וּמַחְשָׁבָה
she'einah tovah hafer uvateil	שֶׁאֵינָה טוֹבָה הָפֵר וּבַטֵּל
atzato kedichtiv "utzu etzah	עֵצָתוֹ כְּדִכְתִיב עֻצוּ עֵצָה
vetufar dabberu davar velo yakum	וְתֻפָר דַּבְּרוּ דָבָר וְלֹא יָקוּם
ki immanu el" vehaseir mei'ittanu	כִּי עִמָּנוּ אֵל וְהָסֵר מֵאִתָּנוּ
kol machloket, kin'ah, sin'ah	כָּל מַחְלֹקֶת, קִנְאָה, שִׂנְאָה
vetacharut uva'avur shimcha	וְתַחֲרוּת וּבַעֲבוּר שִׁמְךָ
el shaddai bateil mei'aleinu kol	אֵל שַׁדַּי בַּטֵּל מֵעָלֵינוּ כָּל
mastinim umekatregim, bein	מַשְׂטִינִים וּמְקַטְרְגִים, בֵּין
lema'lah bein lemattah, velo	לְמַעְלָה בֵּין לְמַטָּה, וְלֹא
yihyeh bahem koach lehastin	יִהְיֶה בָּהֶם כֹּחַ לְהַשְׂטִין
ulekatreig aleinu. Utetzavveh	וּלְקַטְרֵג עָלֵינוּ. וּתְצַוֶּה
lemal'achecha la'azor lanu	לְמַלְאָכֶיךָ לַעֲזֹר לָנוּ
ulesay'einu kedichtiv lo te'unneh	וּלְסַיְּיעֵנוּ כְּדִכְתִיב לֹא תְאֻנֶּה
eleicha ra'ah venega lo yikrav	אֵלֶיךָ רָעָה וְנֶגַע לֹא יִקְרַב
be'oholecha ki mal'achav	בְּאָהֳלֶךָ כִּי מַלְאָכָיו
yetzavveh lach lishmarecha	יְצַוֶּה לָּךְ לִשְׁמָרֶךָ
bechol derachecha.	בְּכָל דְּרָכֶיךָ.
Anna adonai el rachum	אָנָּא יְיָ אֵל רַחוּם
vechannun erech appayim	וְחַנּוּן אֶרֶךְ אַפַּיִם
verav chesed ve'emet yotzer	וְרַב חֶסֶד וֶאֱמֶת יוֹצֵר
or uvorei choshech, oseh	אוֹר וּבוֹרֵא חֹשֶׁךְ, עֹשֶׂה
shalom uvorei et hakkol, al yihyu	שָׁלוֹם וּבוֹרֵא אֶת הַכֹּל, אַל יִהְיוּ
avonoteinu mone'im hattov	עֲוֹנוֹתֵינוּ מוֹנְעִים הַטּוֹב
mei'ittanu, vetatteh et libboteinu	מֵאִתָּנוּ, וְתַטֶּה אֶת לִבּוֹתֵנוּ
shenchabbeid echad et hasheini,	שֶׁנְּכַבֵּד אֶחָד אֶת הַשֵּׁנִי,
vetashreh et shechinatecha	וְתַשְׁרֶה אֶת שְׁכִינָתְךָ
beineinu, veyihyu beineinu	בֵּינֵינוּ, וְיִהְיוּ בֵּינֵינוּ
ahavah ve'achavah, shalom	אַהֲבָה וְאַחֲוָה, שָׁלוֹם

verei'ut ve'orah vesimchah
mei'attah ve'ad olam. Vekayyeim
banu et hakkatuv "hassam
gevuleich shalom cheilev chittim
yasbi'eich" ve'et hakkatuv "yehi
shalom becheilech shalvah
be'armenotayich."

וְרֵעוּת וְאוֹרָה וְשִׂמְחָה
מֵעַתָּה וְעַד עוֹלָם. וְקַיֵּם
בָּנוּ אֶת הַכָּתוּב הַשָּׂם
גְּבוּלֵךְ שָׁלוֹם חֵלֶב חִטִּים
יַשְׂבִּיעֵךְ וְאֶת הַכָּתוּב יְהִי
שָׁלוֹם בְּחֵילֵךְ שַׁלְוָה
בְּאַרְמְנוֹתָיִךְ.

Uvarecheini na bivrachah
hakketuvah betoratecha:
"yevarech'cha adonai
veyishmerecha, ya'eir adonai
panav elecha vichunnekka, yissa
adonai panav elecha veyaseim
lecha shalom," vehitmallei
berachamim gedolim aleinu
umalei kol mish'alot libbeinu
letovah velivrachah vekayeim
beva'ali et hakkatuv "ve'attah
shalom uveit'cha shalom vechol
asher lecha shalom" ve'et
hakkatuv "venachah alav ruach
adonai, ruach chochmah uvinah,
ruach eitzah ugevurah, ruach da'at
veyir'at adonai," amen chen yehi
ratzon netzach selah va'ed.

וּבָרְכֵנִי נָא בִּבְרָכָה
הַכְּתֻבָה בְּתוֹרָתֶךְ:
יְבָרֶכְךָ יְיָ
וְיִשְׁמְרֶךָ, יָאֵר יְיָ
פָּנָיו אֵלֶיךָ וִיחֻנֶּךָּ, יִשָּׂא
יְיָ פָּנָיו אֵלֶיךָ וְיָשֵׂם
לְךָ שָׁלוֹם, וְהִתְמַלֵּא
בְּרַחֲמִים גְּדוֹלִים עָלֵינוּ
וּמַלֵּא כָּל מִשְׁאֲלוֹת לִבֵּנוּ
לְטוֹבָה וְלִבְרָכָה וְקַיֵּם
בְּבַעֲלִי אֶת הַכָּתוּב וְאַתָּה
שָׁלוֹם וּבֵיתְךָ שָׁלוֹם וְכֹל
אֲשֶׁר לְךָ שָׁלוֹם וְאֶת
הַכָּתוּב וְנָחָה עָלָיו רוּחַ
יְיָ, רוּחַ חָכְמָה וּבִינָה,
רוּחַ עֵצָה וּגְבוּרָה, רוּחַ דַּעַת
וְיִרְאַת יְיָ, אָמֵן כֵּן יְהִי
רָצוֹן נֶצַח סֶלָה וָעֶד.

Adonai oz le'ammo yittein adonai
yevarech et ammo vashalom.
Yihyu leratzon imrei fi vehegyon
libbi lefanecha, adonai tzuri
vego'ali.

יְיָ עֹז לְעַמּוֹ יִתֵּן יְיָ
יְבָרֵךְ אֶת עַמּוֹ בַשָּׁלוֹם.
יִהְיוּ לְרָצוֹן אִמְרֵי פִי וְהֶגְיוֹן
לִבִּי לְפָנֶיךָ, יְיָ צוּרִי
וְגֹאֲלִי.

Adonai tzeva'ot immanu misgav
lanu elohei ya'akov selah, adonai
tzeva'ot ashrei adam botei'ach
bach, adonai hoshi'ah hammelech
ya'aneinu veyom kare'einu.

יְיָ צְבָאוֹת עִמָּנוּ מִשְׂגָּב
לָנוּ אֱלֹהֵי יַעֲקֹב סֶלָה, יְיָ
צְבָאוֹת אַשְׁרֵי אָדָם בֹּטֵחַ
בָּךְ, יְיָ הוֹשִׁיעָה הַמֶּלֶךְ
יַעֲנֵנוּ בְיוֹם קָרְאֵנוּ.

Notes

Prayer for Fertility

T HE FOLLOWING IS a prayer for those wishing to have children, written by the great medieval sage Nachmanides. The prayer is a heartfelt plea to God not only for a child, but for the blessing of righteous, healthy and successful offspring who embody purity, beauty, and goodness.

May it be Your will, Rock of all the worlds, Righteous in all generations, for the sake of Your great name that emerges from the verse "The Lord will remember us; He will bless," that You grant me offspring, holy seed, desirable and proper, good and beautiful, well-formed and accepted, and fit to live and exist without sin and transgression. Bless me with Your name and bless my home with offspring, and let me know that my tent is in peace. Draw the lineage of my seed and all my sources from the origin of Israel, and purify my body, sanctify my soul, my thoughts, my intellect, my knowledge, and all my feelings. Strengthen me, fortify me, and clothe me with Your good, pure, and generous spirit, with the intention of my supplication, so that I may fulfill Your will, and my offspring shall be built, live, be refined, and act truly and uprightly, and draw and be fashioned and stand in his place of success.

Help me be prepared to complete this child, to establish him and make him stand in grace, kindness, strength, health, vigor, might, and bravery. Have mercy on him in his formation, in his development and growth, in his being and creation, in his formation, with his soul, spirit, and breath. Let there be no damage or deficiency in him or in any of his limbs, no impact or incident, no illness or suffering, no pain or sorrow, no affliction or disease, no illness and no need for healing, and let him lack no good all the days of his life. Bless me, my home, and my seed in all things that complete our understanding, our intellect, and our feelings to do all deeds according to Your will, and bless us with the blessings of the heavens above, the blessings of the deep that lies beneath, and with Your blessings let the house of Your servant be blessed forever, amen, forever, selah.

Yehi ratzon millefanecha tzur	יְהִי רָצוֹן מִלְפָנֶיךָ צוּר
kol ha'olamim tzaddik bechol	כָּל הָעוֹלָמִים צַדִּיק בְּכָל
haddorot, lema'an shimcha	הַדּוֹרוֹת, לְמַעַן שִׁמְךָ
haggadol hayyotzei mippasuk	הַגָּדוֹל הַיּוֹצֵא מִפָּסוּק
adonai zacharnu yevareich,	ה׳ זְכָרָנוּ יְבָרֵךְ,
shettittein li zera chadash zera	שֶׁתִּתֵּן לִי זֶרַע
kodesh, ratzui vehagun tov	חָדָשׁ זֶרַע קֹדֶשׁ, רָצוּי וְהָגוּן טוֹב
veyafeh metukkan umekubbal,	וְיָפֶה מְתֻקָּן וּמְקֻבָּל,
vera'ui lichyot ulehitkayyeim beli	וְרָאוּי לִחְיוֹת וּלְהִתְקַיֵּם בְּלִי
avon ve'ashmah, utevarecheini	עָוֹן וְאַשְׁמָה, וּתְבָרְכֵנִי
beshimcha utevareich et	בִּשְׁמְךָ וּתְבָרֵךְ אֶת
beiti bizcharim, ve'eida ki	בֵּיתִי בִּזְכָרִים, וְאֵדַע כִּי
shalom oholi. Vetimshoch	שָׁלוֹם אָהֳלִי. וְתִמְשֹׁךְ
meshech zar'ei vechol	מֶשֶׁךְ זַרְעִי וְכָל
ma'aynei mimmekor yisrael,	מַעֲיָנֵי מִמְּקוֹר יִשְׂרָאֵל,
vetaher gufi vekaddeish nafshi	וְטַהֵר גּוּפִי וְקַדֵּשׁ נַפְשִׁי
umachshevotai vesichli veda'ti	וּמַחְשְׁבוֹתַי וְשִׂכְלִי וְדַעְתִּי
veyeter hargashotai, etchazzeik	וְיֶתֶר הַרְגָּשׁוֹתַי, אֶתְחַזֵּק
ve'et'ammeitz ve'etlabbeish	וְאֶתְאַמֵּץ וְאֶתְלַבֵּשׁ
beruchacha hattovah hazzakkah	בְּרוּחֲךָ הַטּוֹבָה הַזַּכָּה
vehannedivah bechavvanat	וְהַנְּדִיבָה בְּכַוָּנַת
techinnati, kedei she'ashlim	תְּחִנָּתִי, כְּדֵי שֶׁאַשְׁלִים
retzonecha, vetashlim zar'i	רְצוֹנֶךָ, וְתַשְׁלִים זַרְעִי
veyivneh veyichyeh veyitztayyeir	וְיִבָּנֶה וְיִחְיֶה וְיִצְטַיֵּר
veya'aseh be'emet veyosher,	וְיֵעָשֶׂה בֶּאֱמֶת וְיֹשֶׁר,
veyimmasheich veyuttach	וְיִמָּשֵׁךְ וְיֻתַּךְ

veya'amod bimkom hatzlachato.

וְיַעֲמֹד בִּמְקוֹם הַצְלָחָתוֹ.

Utechonein kol hana'otai
kedei lehashlimo ulekayyemo
uleha'amido beta'am bechein
bechesed bechoach bivri'ut
be'ometz uvechozek uvetokef
bigvurah. Uterachem alav
behe'asuto behitrakkemo
behitmattecho behitlabbesho
vehitzigatto al burav al mechono
behoyato uvivri'ato bitzirato
ba'asiyyato, benafsho berucho
uvenishmato, bikrovav uvitzurav,
velo yehei bo velo be'echad
me'eivarav lo nezek velo chesron
lo paga velo mikreh lo choli velo
madveh lo ke'eiv velo tza'ar lo
naga velo machalah, lo choli velo
rifyon, velo yechsar kol tuv kol
yemei chayyav. Utevarecheini
ani uveiti vezar'i bechol
davar hammashlim da'teinu
vesichleinu veharegashoteinu
la'asot kol ma'asim lirtzonecha,
utevarecheinu birchot shamayim
mei'al birchot tehom rovetzet
tachat, umibbirchotecha yevorach
beit avdecha le'olam, amen
netzach selah

וּתְכוֹנֵן כָּל הֲנָאוֹתַי
כְּדֵי לְהַשְׁלִימוֹ וּלְקַיְּמוֹ
וּלְהַעֲמִידוֹ בְּטַעַם בָּחֵן
בְּחֶסֶד בְּכֹחַ בִּבְרִיאוּת
בְּאֹמֶץ וּבְחֹזֶק וּבְתֹקֶף
בִּגְבוּרָה. וּתְרַחֵם עָלָיו
בְּהֵעָשׂוֹתוֹ בְּהִתְרַקְּמוֹ
בְּהִתְמַתְּחוֹ בְּהִתְלַבְּשׁוֹ
וְהַצִּיגַתּוֹ עַל בּוּרָיו עַל מְכוֹנוֹ
בְּהֱיוֹתוֹ וּבְבְרִיאָתוֹ בִּיצִירָתוֹ
בַּעֲשִׂיָּתוֹ, בְּנַפְשׁוֹ בְּרוּחוֹ
וּבְנִשְׁמָתוֹ, בְּקִרְבָיו וּבְיצוּרָיו,
וְלֹא יְהֵא בּוֹ וְלֹא בְּאֶחָד
מֵאֵבָרָיו לֹא נֶזֶק וְלֹא חֶסָרוֹן
לֹא פָּגַע וְלֹא מִקְרֶה לֹא חֹלִי וְלֹא
מַדְוֶה לֹא כְּאֵב וְלֹא צַעַר לֹא
נָגַע וְלֹא מַחֲלָה, לֹא חֹלִי וְלֹא
רִפְיוֹן, וְלֹא יֶחְסַר כָּל טוֹב כָּל
יְמֵי חַיָּיו. וּתְבָרְכֵנִי
אֲנִי וּבֵיתִי וְזַרְעִי בְּכָל
דָּבָר הַמַּשְׁלִים דַּעְתֵּנוּ
וְשִׂכְלֵנוּ וְהַרְגָּשׁוֹתֵנוּ
לַעֲשׂוֹת כָּל מַעֲשִׂים לִרְצוֹנֶךָ,
וּתְבָרְכֵנוּ בְּרְכַּת שָׁמַיִם
מֵעַל בְּרְכַּת תְּהוֹם רֹבֶצֶת
תָּחַת, וּמִבְרכוֹתֶיךָ יְבֹרַךְ
בֵּית עַבְדְּךָ לְעוֹלָם, אָמֵן
נֶצַח סֶלָה

Expectant Mother's Prayer

T HIS PRAYER IS a sincere plea to be said during pregnancy, seeking the Almighty's grace to alleviate the challenges and pain associated with childbearing. It asks for the blessings of a safe and healthy pregnancy and delivery, as well as a healthy, peaceful, and blessed life for the unborn child.

May it be Your will before You, Lord, my God and the God of my forefathers, that You remove from me the pain of pregnancy and add and give me strength and vigor throughout the days of pregnancy, that my strength and the strength of the fetus not be depleted in any way in the world. Deliver me from Eve's enticement and from the curse "I will greatly increase your pain in childbirth; in pain you will give birth to children," and may it be that when the time of my delivery arrives, my labor pains will not turn against me, and the child will enter the world swiftly and easily, without any harm to me or the child. May the child be born at a good hour and with good fortune, to life, peace, and health, to grace and kindness, to wealth and honor, and may the verse be fulfilled in me: "There shall be no miscarriage or barrenness in your land; I will fill the number of your days."

May my husband and I raise him for Your service and in the ways of Your holy Bible, for a good life, peace, wealth, happiness, honor, and rest, and let neither I nor the unborn be shaken, not in body, not in limbs, not in veins, not in tendons, not in skin and flesh or any other human construction, neither within the body cavity nor outside the body cavity. Strengthen my strength, my spirit, and my bones, as it is said: "It will be healing to your flesh and refreshment to your bones."

For You, Lord, I have hoped; You will answer, Lord my God. I will rejoice in the Lord; I will exult in the God of my salvation. Lord, please save me; hurry to my help, Lord. Hurry to my help, Lord, my salvation. I have hoped for Your salvation, Lord. Hear, Lord, my voice when I call; be gracious to me and answer me. Do it for the sake of our holy forefathers, and for the sake of their merit and righteousness, and for the sake of their Torah and their good deeds, those who dwell in the dust here and all over the world. Remember their love and revive their offspring and deliver them from death, miscarriage, and from all illness and plague.

Bless me as You have promised us in Your holy Bible through Moses Your servant, from the mouth of Your glory, as it is said: "And I will love you and bless you and multiply you; I will bless the fruit of your womb and the fruit of your soil, your grain and your new wine and your oil, the calves of your herds and the lambs of your flocks in the land that I swore to your forefathers to give you. You will be blessed above all peoples; there will be no male or female barren among you or among your livestock." So bless me and answer me and prolong my days in pleasantness, as it is said: "With long life I will satisfy him and show him My salvation," amen.

Yehi ratzon millefanecha adonai'	יְהִי רָצוֹן מִלְּפָנֶיךָ ה'
elohai veilohei avotai, shettakeil	אֱלֹהַי וֵאלֹהֵי אֲבוֹתַי, שֶׁתָּקֵל
mei'alai et tza'ar ibburi vetosif	מֵעָלַי אֶת צַעַר עִבּוּרִי וְתוֹסִיף
vetitten li koach ve'on bechol	וְתִתֶּן לִי כֹּחַ וְאוֹן בְּכָל
yemei ha'ibbur, shello yutash	יְמֵי הָעִבּוּר, שֶׁלֹּא יִתַּשׁ
kochi velo koach ha'ubar beshum	כֹּחִי וְלֹא כֹּחַ הָעֻבָּר
davar shebba'olam, vetatzil oti	בְּשׁוּם דָּבָר שֶׁבָּעוֹלָם,
mippitkah shel chavvah umikkil'lat	וְתַצִּיל אוֹתִי מִפִּתְקָה שֶׁל
"harbah arbeh etzevoneich	חַוָּה וּמִקְלְלַת "הַרְבָּה
veheironeich, be'etzev tel'di	אַרְבֶּה עִצְּבוֹנֵךְ וְהֵרֹנֵךְ,
banim", vai'hi	בְּעֶצֶב תֵּלְדִי בָנִים", וַיְהִי

be'eit leidati ki yimle'u yemai
laledet, lo yehappechu alai
tzirai, veyeutzeu havvalad l'avir
ha'olam berega katan, bekallut,
beli shum hezzeik lo li velo
lavv'lad, veyihyeh nolad besha'ah
tovah uvemazzal tov, lechayyim
uleshalom velivri'ut, lechein
ulechesed, le'osher ul'kkavod,
vikuyam bi mikra shekkatuv: "lo
tihyeh meshakkeilah va'akarah
be'artzecha et mispar yamecha
amallei," va'ani uva'ali nigd'leihu
la'avodatecha uletoratecha
hakkedoshah, ulechayyim tovim
uleshalom ve'osher ve'osher
vechavod umenuchah, velo
nihyeh lo ani velo ha'ubar
nizzokim, lo bagguf velo
be'eivarim velo be'orekim velo
begidim velo be'or uvasar
ushe'ar kol binyan benei
adam, lo betoch chalal hagguf
velo chutz lechallal hagguf,
vetechazak et kochi veruchi
ve'atzmotai, kemo shenne'emar:
"rif'ut tehi lesharrecha veshikkui
le'atzmotecha".

Ki lecha adonai' hochalti attah
ma'aneh adonai' elohai. Va'ani
badonai e'lozah agilah belohei
yish'i. Retzei adonai' lehatzileini,

בְּעֵת לֵידָתִי כִּי יִמְלְאוּ יְמֵי
לָלֶדֶת, לֹא יְהָפְכוּ עָלַי
צִירַי, וְיֵצֵא הַוָּלָד לַאֲוִיר
הָעוֹלָם בְּרֶגַע קָטָן, בְּקַלּוּת,
בְּלִי שׁוּם הֶזֵּק לֹא לִי וְלֹא
לַוָּלָד, וְיִהְיֶה נוֹלָד בְּשָׁעָה
טוֹבָה וּבְמַזָּל טוֹב, לְחַיִּים
וּלְשָׁלוֹם וְלִבְרִיאוּת, לְחֵן
וּלְחֶסֶד, לְעוֹשֶׁר וּלְכָבוֹד,
וְיִקָיַּם בִּי מִקְרָא שֶׁכָּתוּב: " לֹא
תִהְיֶה מְשַׁכֵּלָה וַעֲקָרָה
בְּאַרְצֶךָ אֶת מִסְפַּר יָמֶיךָ
אֲמַלֵּא", וַאֲנִי וּבַעֲלִי נְגִדְּלֵהוּ
לַעֲבוֹדָתְךָ וּלְתוֹרָתְךָ
הַקְּדוֹשָׁה, וּלְחַיִּים טוֹבִים
וּלְשָׁלוֹם וְעוֹשֶׁר וְאוֹשֶׁר
וְכָבוֹד וּמְנוּחָה, וְלֹא
נִהְיֶה לֹא אֲנִי וְלֹא הָעֻבָּר
נִזוֹקִים, לֹא בַּגּוּף וְלֹא
בָּאֵבָרִים וְלֹא בָּעוֹרְקִים וְלֹא
בְּגִידִים וְלֹא בָּעוֹר וּבַשָׂר
וּשְׁאָר כָּל בִּנְיַן בְּנֵי
אָדָם, לֹא בְּתוֹךְ חֲלַל הַגּוּף
וְלֹא חוּץ לְחַלַל הַגּוּף,
וְתֶחֱזַק אֶת כֹּחִי וְרוּחִי
וְעַצְמוֹתַי, כְּמוֹ שֶׁנֶּאֱמַר:
"רְפְאוּת תְּהִי לְשָׁרֶךָ וְשִׁקּוּי
לְעַצְמוֹתֶיךָ".

כִּי לְךָ ה' הוֹחָלְתִּי אַתָּה
מַעֲנֶה ה' אֱלֹהָי. וַאֲנִי
בַה' אֶעֱלוֹזָה אָגִילָה בֵּאלֹהֵי
יִשְׁעִי. רְצֵה ה' לְהַצִּילֵנִי,

adonai le'ezrati chushah.
Chushah le'ezrati adonai teshu'ati.
Lishu'atecha kivviti adonai'. Shema
adonai koli ekra vechanneini
va'aneini. Aseih lema'an avoteinu
hakkedoshim, ulema'an zechutam
vetzidkatam, ulema'an toratam
uma'aseihem hattovim shel
shochenei afar hattemunim poh
uvechol ha'olam. Tizkor ahavatam
utechayeh zar'am vetatzil otam
mimmavet umimmeshakkelet
umikkol choli umaddeveh.

Utivarcheini ka'asher havtachtanu
betoratecha hakkedoshah
al yedei mosheh avdecha,
mippi kevodecha ka'amur:
"va'aheivecha uveirach'cha
vehirbecha, uveirach peri vitnecha
uferi admatecha degan'cha
vetirosh'cha veyitzharecha
shegar alafecha ve'ashterot
tzonecha al ha'adamah asher
nishba la'avotecha latet lach.
Baruch tihyeh mikkol ha'ammim,
lo yihyeh vecha akar va'akarah
uvivhemtecha". Ken tivar'cheini
veta'aneini veta'arich yamai
banne'imim, ka'amur: "orech
yamim asbi'eihu ve'ar'eihu
bishu'ati", amen.

ה׳ לְעֶזְרָתִי חוּשָׁה. חוּשָׁה
לְעֶזְרָתִי ה׳ תְּשׁוּעָתִי.
לִישׁוּעָתְךָ קִוִּיתִי ה׳. שְׁמַע
ה׳ קוֹלִי אֶקְרָא וְחָנֵּנִי
וַעֲנֵנִי. עֲשֵׂה לְמַעַן אֲבוֹתֵינוּ
הַקְּדוֹשִׁים, וּלְמַעַן זְכוּתָם
וְצִדְקָתָם, וּלְמַעַן תּוֹרָתָם
וּמַעֲשֵׂיהֶם הַטּוֹבִים שֶׁל
שׁוֹכְנֵי עָפָר הַטְּמוּנִים פֹּה
וּבְכָל הָעוֹלָם. תִּזְכּוֹר אַהֲבָתָם
וּתְחַיֶּה זַרְעָם וְתַצִּיל אוֹתָם
מִמָּוֶת וּמִמְּשַׁכֶּלֶת
וּמִכָּל חֹלִי וּמַדְוֶה.

וּתְבָרְכֵנִי כַּאֲשֶׁר הִבְטַחְתָּנוּ
בְּתוֹרָתְךָ הַקְּדוֹשָׁה
עַל יְדֵי מֹשֶׁה עַבְדֶּךָ,
מִפִּי כְבוֹדֶךָ כָּאָמוּר:
״וַאֲהֵבְךָ וּבֵרַכְךָ
וְהִרְבֶּךָ, וּבֵרַךְ פְּרִי בִטְנְךָ
וּפְרִי אַדְמָתֶךָ דְּגָנְךָ
וְתִירֹשְׁךָ וְיִצְהָרֶךָ
שְׁגַר אֲלָפֶיךָ וְעַשְׁתְּרוֹת
צֹאנֶךָ עַל הָאֲדָמָה אֲשֶׁר
נִשְׁבַּע לַאֲבֹתֶיךָ לָתֶת לָךְ.
בָּרוּךְ תִּהְיֶה מִכָּל הָעַמִּים,
לֹא יִהְיֶה בְךָ עָקָר וַעֲקָרָה
וּבִבְהֶמְתֶּךָ״. כֵּן תְּבָרְכֵנִי
וְתַעֲנֵנִי וְתַאֲרִיךְ יָמַי
בַּנְּעִימִים, כָּאָמוּר: ״אֹרֶךְ
יָמִים אַשְׂבִּיעֵהוּ וְאַרְאֵהוּ
בִּישׁוּעָתִי״, אָמֵן.

Prayer for the Success of One's Children

As parents, our deepest hopes and prayers often center around the well-being and success of our children. In this prayer, we seek divine guidance for our children's path in life, hoping they live enriching lives that glorify God's name, maintain good health, and possess noble character traits. We ask for their success and protection, and that our efforts as parents enable us to support and raise them in joy and peace.

Master of the Universe: Grant that our children shine in Bible study, be healthy in body and mind, possess good character traits, and engage in the study of the Bible for its own sake. Bless them with long and good lives, filled with the study of the Bible, wisdom, and reverence for Heaven. May they be beloved above and delightful below. Protect them from the evil eye, the evil inclination, and all kinds of suffering, and grant them healthy senses for Your service. Bestow upon us, in Your abundant mercy, (and upon my wife / and upon my husband), that our days be filled with longevity, goodness, pleasantness, love, and peace. May we merit to raise each of our sons and each of our daughters to follow in the ways of the Bible, to have a successful marriage and to perfom good deeds.

Arrange for each of my sons his intended spouse and for each of my daughters her intended husband, and let them not be rejected in favor of others, God forbid. Bless the work of our hands to give them a dowry and gifts generously, and enable us to fulfill what we promise to give them without a vow, and to marry them off with their spouses in their youth peacefully, with ease, and joyfully, and from them will emerge good fruits and righteous children, bringing merit to us and our families.

Let not Your great name be desecrated through us or our offspring, God forbid. Fulfill all the desires of our heart for good in health, success, and all that is good. May the glory of Your great name and the honor of Your Bible be exalted through us, our offspring, and the offspring of our offspring. Amen, may it be Your will. May the words of my mouth and the meditation of my heart be acceptable before You, O Lord, my rock and my redeemer.

Ribbono shel olam: zakkeinu	רִבּוֹנוֹ שֶׁל עוֹלָם: זַכֵּנוּ
sheyyihyu baneinu me'irim	שֶׁיִּהְיוּ בָּנֵינוּ מְאִירִים
battorah, veyihyu beri'im begufam	בַּתּוֹרָה, וְיִהְיוּ בְּרִיאִים בְּגוּפָם
vesichlam, ba'alei middot	וְשִׂכְלָם, בַּעֲלֵי מִדּוֹת
tovot, osekim battorah lishmah.	טוֹבוֹת, עוֹסְקִים בַּתּוֹרָה לִשְׁמָהּ.
Vetein lahem chayyim arukkim	וְתֵן לָהֶם חַיִּים אֲרֻכִּים
vetovim, veyihyu memulla'im	וְטוֹבִים, וְיִהְיוּ מְמֻלָּאִים
battorah uvechochmah	בַּתּוֹרָה וּבְחָכְמָה
uveyir'at shamayim, veyihyu	וּבְיִרְאַת שָׁמַיִם, וְיִהְיוּ
ahuvim lema'lah venechmadim	אֲהוּבִים לְמַעְלָה וְנֶחְמָדִים
lemattah. Vetatzileim mei'ayin	לְמַטָּה. וְתַצִּילֵם מֵעַיִן
hara umiyyetzer hara umikkol	הָרַע וּמִיֵּצֶר הָרַע וּמִכָּל
minei pur'anuyot, veyihyu lahem	מִינֵי פֻּרְעָנֻיוֹת, וְיִהְיוּ לָהֶם
chushim beri'im la'avodatecha.	חוּשִׁים בְּרִיאִים לַעֲבוֹדָתֶךָ.
Vezakkeinu berachamecha	וְזַכֵּנוּ בְּרַחֲמֶיךָ
harabbim, (ve'et ishti, ve'et ba'ali),	הָרַבִּים, (וְאֶת אִשְׁתִּי, וְאֶת בַּעֲלִי),
shettemallei mispar yameinu	שֶׁתְּמַלֵּא מִסְפַּר יָמֵינוּ
ba'arichut yamim veshanim	בַּאֲרִיכוּת יָמִים וְשָׁנִים בַּטּוֹב
battov uvanne'imim, ve'ahavah	וּבַנְּעִימִים, וְאַהֲבָה וְשָׁלוֹם,
veshalom, venizkeh legaddel kol	וְנִזְכֶּה לְגַדֵּל כָּל
echad mibbanai vechol achat	אֶחָד מִבָּנַי וְכָל אַחַת

mibbenotai letorah, lechuppah
ulema'asim tovim.

Vetazmin lechol echad mibbanai
et bat ziyuvvgo ulechol achat
mibbenotai et ben ziyuvvgah,
velo yudd'chu lifnei acheirim chas
veshalom. Uvareich ma'aseih
yadeinu littein lahem mohar
umattan be'ayin yafah, venuchal
lekayyeim mah she'anu mavtichim
litten lahem beli neder, ulehasi'am
im zivvugam biymei hanne'urim
benachat uverevach uvesimchah,
umeheim yeitze'u peirot tovim
uvanim tzaddikim zochim
umezakkim lechol yisra'eil.

Velo yitchalel shimcha haggadol
al yadeinu, velo al yedei
zar'einu chas veshalom umallei
kol mish'alot libbeinu letovah
bivri'ut, behatzlachah vechol
tuv, veyitgaddiel kevod shimcha
haggadol vechavod toratecha
al yadeinu ve'al yedei zar'einu
vezera zar'einu, amein kein yehi
ratzon. Yihyu leratzon imrei fi
vehegyon libbi lefanecha adonai
tzuri vego'ali.

מִבְּנוֹתַי לְתוֹרָה, לְחֻפָּה
וּלְמַעֲשִׂים טוֹבִים.

וְתַזְמִין לְכָל אֶחָד מִבָּנַי
אֶת בַּת זִיוּגוֹ וּלְכָל אַחַת
מִבְּנוֹתַיי אֶת בֶּן זִיוּנָהּ,
וְלֹא יִדָּחוּ לִפְנֵי אֲחֵרִים
חַס וְשָׁלוֹם. וּבָרֵךְ
מַעֲשֶׂה יָדֵינוּ לִתֵּן לָהֶם
מֹהַר וּמַתָּן בְּעַיִן יָפָה,
וְנוּכַל לְקַיֵּם מַה שֶׁאָנוּ
מַבְטִיחִים לִתֵּן לָהֶם בְּלִי נֶדֶר,
וּלְהַשִּׂיאָם עִם זִיוּנָם בְּימֵי
הַנְּעוּרִים בְּנַחַת וּבְרֶוַח
וּבְשִׂמְחָה, וּמֵהֶם יֵצְאוּ
פֵּרוֹת טוֹבִים וּבָנִים צַדִּיקִים
זוֹכִים וּמְזַכִּים לְכָל יִשְׂרָאֵל.

וְלֹא יִתְחַלֵּל שִׁמְךָ הַגָּדוֹל
עַל יָדֵינוּ, וְלֹא עַל יְדֵי
זַרְעֵנוּ חַס וְשָׁלוֹם וּמַלֵּא
כָּל מִשְׁאֲלוֹת לִבֵּנוּ לְטוֹבָה
בִּבְרִיאוּת, בְּהַצְלָחָה וְכָל
טוּב, וְיִתְגַּדֵּל כְּבוֹד שִׁמְךָ
הַגָּדוֹל וְכָבוֹד תּוֹרָתֶךָ
עַל יָדֵינוּ וְעַל יְדֵי זַרְעֵנוּ
וְזֶרַע זַרְעֵנוּ, אָמֵן כֵּן יְהִי
רָצוֹן. יִהְיוּ לְרָצוֹן אִמְרֵי פִי
וְהֶגְיוֹן לִבִּי לְפָנֶיךָ ה'
צוּרִי וְגוֹאֲלִי.

Prayer for Oneself and One's Children to Know God

THIS PRAYER IS a humble petition for divine wisdom and the infusion of holiness into our lives and those of our descendants. It seeks the fulfillment of the biblical promise of a spirit enriched with wisdom, understanding, and reverence for God, aspiring for a world where the knowledge of the Divine is as widespread as the seas.

May it be Your will before You, Lord our God and God of our ancestors, who graciously gives knowledge to man, that You bestow wisdom, understanding, and knowledge of holiness upon us and upon all our offspring. And please fulfill in me the verse "and the spirit of the Lord shall rest upon him, the spirit of wisdom and understanding, the spirit of counsel and might, the spirit of knowledge and the fear of the Lord." And may You influence, implant, and establish in the hearts of all our offspring the knowledge of the Bible, the knowledge of holiness, and please also establish this in us, and may the earth be filled with the knowledge of the Lord as the waters cover the sea. Blessed are You, Lord, who graciously gives knowledge.

Yehi ratzon millefanecha adonai	יְהִי רָצוֹן מִלְּפָנֶיךָ יי
eloheinu velohei avoteinu	אֱלֹהֵינוּ וֵאלֹהֵי אֲבוֹתֵינוּ
hachonen le'adam da'at	הַחוֹנֵן לְאָדָם דַּעַת
shettashpia' chochmah binah	שֶׁתַּשְׁפִּיעַ חָכְמָה בִּינָה
veda'at dikdushah aleinu ve'al	וְדַעַת דִּקְדֻשָּׁה עָלֵינוּ וְעַל
kol zarei'nu vekayyam na bi	כָּל זַרְעֵנוּ וְקַיֵּם נָא בִּי
"venachah alav ruach adonai	וְנָחָה עָלָיו רוּחַ יְיָ

ruach chochmah uvinah ruach
eitzah ugevurah ruach da'at
veyir'at adonai" vetashpia'
vetinnata vetikba bileivav
kol zarei'nu da'at torah, da'at
dikdushah vekayyam na banu
"umale'ah ha'aretz dei'ah et
adonai kammayim layyam
mechassim", baruch attah adonai
chonein hadda'at

רוּחַ חָכְמָה וּבִינָה רוּחַ
עֵצָה וּגְבוּרָה רוּחַ דַּעַת
וְיִרְאַת יְיָ וְתַשְׁפִּיעַ
וְתִנָּטֵע וְתִקָּבַע בְּלֵבָב
כָּל זַרְעֵנוּ דַּעַת תּוֹרָה, דַּעַת
דִּקְדוּשָׁה וְקַיָּם נָא בָּנוּ
וּמָלְאָה הָאָרֶץ דֵּעָה אֶת
יְיָ כַּמַּיִם לַיָּם
מְכַסִּים, בָּרוּךְ אַתָּה יְיָ
חוֹנֵן הַדָּעַת

Notes

_____
_____
_____
_____
_____
_____
_____
_____
_____
_____
_____
_____
_____
_____
_____

Prayer for One's Parents

THE FOLLOWING PRAYER, written by Rabbi Natan of Breslov, is a tribute to our parents. We ask God for their health, strength, and prosperity, and recognize their profound impact on our lives. We seek divine guidance to honor them properly and to embody the values they have taught us. In short, it is a plea for their well-being and our ability to continue their legacy with love and respect.

May it be Your will, Lord our God and God of our ancestors, that our fathers and our mothers and we ourselves be healthy and strong to serve You truthfully, and that You bestow upon them and us ample sustenance, with ease, great success, and all that is good, to serve You with truth and joy. And place in our hearts the willingness to listen to the voice of our father and our mother, and save us so that we may honor them always, as is Your good will towards us, and we shall serve You truthfully. May our father and our mother raise us to lives aligned with the Bible, to the wedding canopy, and to good deeds, and may they be successful in health, all goodness, and wealth to give us a dowry and gifts and all goodness with gracious countenance. And may He fulfill all the desires of our hearts for the good.

Our Father in heaven, save us all, including all Your people Israel, and may we merit to magnify the glory of Your great name and the honor of Your Bible always. May the words of my mouth and the meditation of my heart be acceptable before You, Lord, my Rock and my Redeemer.

Yehi ratzon millefanecha adonai
eloheinu vei'elohei avoteinu,

יְהִי רָצוֹן מִלְפָנֶיךָ יהוה
אֱלֹהֵינוּ וֵאלֹהֵי אֲבוֹתֵינוּ,

sheyyihyu avinu ve'immeinu
va'anachnu beri'im vachazakim
la'avod otecha be'emet, vetashpia'
lahem velanu parnasah b'revach
vehatzlachah merubbah vechol
tuv, la'avod otecha be'emet
uvesimchah. Vetein belibbeinu
lishmoa' bekol avinu ve'immeinu,
vehoshi'einu shennechabbeid
otam tamid ka'asher retzonecha
hattov immanu, vena'avod
otecha be'emet, veyigadelu
avinu ve'immeinu otanu letorah
ulechuppah ulema'asim tovim,
veyihyu mutzlachim bivri'ut vechol
tuv va'ashirut litten lanu mohar
umattan vechol tuv beseiver
panim yafot. Umalei kol mish'alot
libbeinu letovah.

Avinu shebbashamayim hoshi'einu
kol zeh bichlal kol ammecha
yisra'eil, venizkeh lehagdil kevod
shimcha haggadol uchevod
toratecha tamid. Yihyu leratzon
imrei-fi vehegyon libbi lefanecha
adonai tzuri vego'ali.

שֶׁיִּהְיוּ אָבִינוּ וְאִמֵּנוּ
וַאֲנַחְנוּ בְּרִיאִים וַחֲזָקִים
לַעֲבֹד אוֹתְךָ בֶּאֱמֶת, וְתַשְׁפִּיעַ
לָהֶם וְלָנוּ פַּרְנָסָה בְּרֶוַח
וְהַצְלָחָה מְרֻבָּה וְכָל
טוּב, לַעֲבֹד אוֹתְךָ בֶּאֱמֶת
וּבְשִׂמְחָה. וְתֵן בְּלִבֵּנוּ
לִשְׁמֹעַ בְּקוֹל אָבִינוּ וְאִמֵּנוּ,
וְהוֹשִׁיעֵנוּ שֶׁנְּכַבֵּד
אוֹתָם תָּמִיד כַּאֲשֶׁר רְצוֹנְךָ
הַטּוֹב עִמָּנוּ, וְנַעֲבֹד
אוֹתְךָ בֶּאֱמֶת, וִינַדְּלוּ
אָבִינוּ וְאִמֵּנוּ אוֹתָנוּ לְתוֹרָה
וּלְחֻפָּה וּלְמַעֲשִׂים טוֹבִים,
וְיִהְיוּ מֻצְלָחִים בִּבְרִיאוּת וְכָל
טוּב וַעֲשִׁירוּת לָתֶן לָנוּ מֹהַר
וּמַתָּן וְכָל טוּב בְּסֵבֶר
פָּנִים יָפוֹת. וּמַלֵּא כָּל מִשְׁאֲלוֹת
לִבֵּנוּ לְטוֹבָה.

אָבִינוּ שֶׁבַּשָּׁמַיִם הוֹשִׁיעֵנוּ
כָּל זֶה בִּכְלָל כָּל עַמְּךָ
יִשְׂרָאֵל, וְנִזְכֶּה לְהַגְדִּיל כְּבוֹד
שִׁמְךָ הַגָּדוֹל וּכְבוֹד
תוֹרָתְךָ תָּמִיד. יְהִי לְרָצוֹן
אִמְרֵי פִי וְהֶגְיוֹן לִבִּי לְפָנֶיךָ
יהוה צוּרִי וְגֹאֲלִי.

Notes

_____

_____

Prayers of Yearning and Repentance

THIS SECTION BRINGS together prayers of deep yearning for God and the earnest journey of repentance, reflecting our soul's desire to forge a closer bond with the Divine. Recognizing that our sins disrupt this sacred connection, we turn to repentance not merely to seek forgiveness and evade punishment but to repair and deepen our relationship with God. Through these prayers, we express our deep longing to transcend our missteps and draw even nearer to the Almighty.

Prayer of Yearning for God

T HE *YEDID NEFESH* prayer, traditionally recited over the Sabbath, is commonly attributed to the sixteenth-century Sephardic Kabbalist, Rabbi Elazar ben Moshe Azikri (1533-1600). It is an intimate prayer of yearning for God's revelation and a profound longing for spiritual intimacy and the protective embrace of God's love.

Beloved of my soul, compassionate Father, draw me, your servant, to your desire. Would that I could run like a gazelle, and bow before Your beauty, for I find your love sweeter than honey or any delight.

Majestic, Beautiful, Radiance of the world, my soul is sick for your love. God, please heal her by bathing her in your serene light - then she shall surely be strengthened and healed and be Your servant forever.

Ancient One, let Your compassion flow. Have pity on the child whom You love -- for I have yearned so long to see your luminescent power. My God, my beloved, hurry; please, do not hide!

Please, my beloved, reveal Yourself. Spread the shelter of your peace over me. May the whole world be illuminated with Your glory; then shall we be glad and rejoice with You. My lover - come quickly, for the time has come - have compassion for me as in days of old.

Yedid nefesh, av harachman,	יְדִיד נֶפֶשׁ, אָב הָרַחֲמָן,
meshoch avdach el-retzonach,	מְשׁוֹךְ עַבְדָּךְ אֶל־רְצוֹנָךְ,
yarutz avdach kemo ayyal,	יָרוּץ עַבְדָּךְ כְּמוֹ אַיָּל,

yishtachaveh mul hadarach, ki
ye'erav-lo yedidutach minnofet
tzuf vechol-ta'am.

Hadur, na'eh, ziv ha'olam, nafshi
cholat ahavatach, anna, eil, na,
refa-na lah behar'ot lah no'am
zivach, az titchazzeik vetitrappei,
vehayetah lach shifchat olam.

Vatik, yehemu rachamecha,
vechus-na al-bein ohavach, ki
zeh kammeh nichsof nichsaf
lir'ot betif'eret uzzach, anna, eili,
machmad libbi, chushah-na ve'al
tit'allam.

Higgaleh-na uferos, chaviv,
alai et-sukkat shelomach, ta'ir
eretz mikkevodach, nagilah
venismechah bach, maher, ahuv,
ki va mo'ed, vechanneini kimei
olam.

יִשְׁתַּחֲוֶה מוּל הֲדָרֵךְ, כִּי
יֶעֱרַב־לוֹ יְדִידוּתֵךְ מִנֹּפֶת
צוּף וְכָל־טָעַם.

הָדוּר, נָאֶה, זִיו הָעוֹלָם, נַפְשִׁי
חוֹלַת אַהֲבָתֵךְ, אָנָּא, אֵל, נָא,
רְפָא־נָא לָהּ בְּהַרְאוֹת לָהּ נֹעַם
זִיוֵךְ, אָז תִּתְחַזֵּק וְתִתְרַפֵּא,
וְהָיְתָה לָךְ שִׁפְחַת עוֹלָם.

וָתִיק, יֶהֱמוּ רַחֲמֶיךָ,
וְחוּס־נָא עַל־בֵּן אוֹהֲבָךְ, כִּי
זֶה כַּמֶּה נִכְסֹף נִכְסַף
לִרְאוֹת בְּתִפְאֶרֶת עֻזָּךְ, אָנָּא, אֵלִי,
מַחְמַד לִבִּי, חוּשָׁה־נָא וְאַל
תִּתְעַלָּם.

הִגָּלֶה־נָא וּפְרֹשׂ, חָבִיב,
עָלַי אֶת־סֻכַּת שְׁלוֹמָךְ, תָּאִיר
אֶרֶץ מִכְּבוֹדָךְ, נָגִילָה
וְנִשְׂמְחָה בָּךְ, מַהֵר, אָהוּב,
כִּי בָא מוֹעֵד, וְחָנֵּנִי כִּימֵי
עוֹלָם.

Notes

_____

_____

_____

_____

Prayer for the Removal of Undesirable Inclinations

RABBI DR. ABRAHAM J. Twerski (1930-2021), a respected rabbi and psychiatrist known for his work with addiction, taught that while we can manage many of our actions and feelings, some are just too tough for us to handle alone. Self-improvement is a journey. We need to put in the effort to better ourselves but also realize when to ask for a little help from above for those stubborn challenges we can't overcome by ourselves.

The following is a prayer for God's help to remove those undesirable traits, inviting divine intervention to aid us in our pursuit of personal growth and inner peace.

May it be Your will before You, Lord our God and God of our ancestors, the great, mighty, and awe-inspiring God, Almighty, exalted and lofty, Who was, Who is, and Who will be, I Will Be Who I Will Be, the Most High God, that You fill me with immense compassion for my body, my soul, my spirit, and my breath, and remove from me all bad traits and all undesirable tendencies, and let not the forces of impurity dominate me. May it please You, Lord, to rescue me, Lord, come quickly to my aid. And save me, Lord my God, from evil thoughts and from all sin, transgression, and iniquity as it is written: "You are my hiding place; you will protect me from trouble and surround me with songs of deliverance. Selah."

Master of the Universe, the sages, your servants of blessed memory wrote: "The eye sees and the heart covets and the instruments of action complete the sin." And also: "There is no guardian for sexual immorality." And it is revealed and known before You that the evil inclination is founded on fire and I am but flesh and blood, and if You do not help me, I do not have the strength to withstand it. Therefore, may it be Your will before You, Lord our God and God of our ancestors, that You assist me and grant me will, wisdom, understanding, knowledge, strength and ability so that I do not follow my heart and my eyes, as it is written: "Turn my eyes away from worthless things; preserve my life according to your way." And grant me the ability to set boundaries for myself so that I do not transgress, and let my heart be steadfast and committed in my hand: "Create in me a pure heart, O God, and renew a steadfast spirit within me": for I have hoped in You, You will answer, Lord my God. Bless me, my Father, and remove from me all sorrow and sighing, and bestow upon me light, joy, holiness, and purity, and clothe me with a good spirit, and a generous spirit will support me, and fulfill in me: "and the spirit of the Lord will rest on him, the spirit of wisdom and understanding, the spirit of counsel and might, the spirit of knowledge and fear of the Lord." And command Your holy and pure angels, who are appointed over the opening of the heart, that they open my heart to Your Bible, as it is written: "Open my eyes that I may see wonderful things in your law": "for the Lord gives wisdom; from his mouth comes knowledge and understanding": Blessed are You, Lord, teach me Your decrees. And fill my heart and the hearts of all Your people, with Your love and fear, and with the love of Your holy Bible and the love of Israel, Your people. And increase, magnify, and multiply the boundary of holiness in Your people, and the house of Israel, and incline my heart and the hearts of all Your people, and the house of Israel, to walk in the way of the Bible and the commandments, holiness and purity, and fulfill in us: "and this is My covenant with them, says the Lord, My spirit that is upon you and My words that I have put in your mouth will not depart from your mouth, or from the mouths of your descendants, or from the mouths of their descendants, says *the Lord, from now on and forever." And also: "for the earth will be filled with the knowledge of the Lord as the waters cover the sea." Amen, so may it be Your will forever and ever.*

And in Your Bible it is written, saying: "Hear, O Israel: The Lord our God, the Lord is one."

May the Lord our God be with us as He was with our ancestors; may He not leave us nor forsake us, to incline our hearts to Him, to walk in all His ways and to keep His commandments, His decrees, and His laws, which He commanded our ancestors. And may these words of mine, which I have pleaded before the Lord, be near to the Lord our God day and night, that He may uphold the cause of His servant and the cause of His people Israel as each day requires, so that all the peoples of the earth may know that the Lord is God and there is no other.

To You, Lord, I call, and to the Lord, I plead for mercy: The earth yields its harvest; God, our God, blesses us.

The Lord Almighty is with us; the God of Jacob is our fortress, Selah. Blessed are those who trust in You, O Lord of hosts; save us, the King will answer us on the day we call.

May the words of my mouth and the meditation of my heart be pleasing in your sight, Lord, my Rock, and my Redeemer.

Yehi ratzon millefanecha adonai	יְהִי רָצוֹן מִלְפָנֶיךָ יְיָ
eloheinu ve'elohai avoteinu, ha'eil	אֱלֹהֵינוּ וֵאלֹהַי אֲבוֹתֵינוּ, הָאֵל
haggadol haggibbor vehannora,	הַגָּדוֹל הַגִּבּוֹר וְהַנּוֹרָא,
el shaddai ram venissa, hayah	אֵל שַׁדַּי רָם וְנִשָּׂא, הָיָה
hoveh veyihyeh, eheyeh asher	הֹוֶה וְיִהְיֶה, אֶהְיֶה אֲשֶׁר
eheyeh, el elyon, shettitmallei	אֶהְיֶה, אֵל עֶלְיוֹן, שֶׁתִּתְמַלֵּא

berachamim atzumim al gufi,
nafshi, ruchi venishmati vehaseir
mittochi kol middot ra'ot vechol
netiyyot she'einan retzuyot ve'al
yishletu bi kochot hattum'ah:
retzeih adonai lehatzileini adonai
le'ezrati chushah. Vehatzileini
adonai elohai mimmachshavot
ra'ot umikkol cheit avon ufesha
kedichtiv: attah seter li mitzar
titzereini rannei falleit tesoveveini
selah.

Ribbono shel olam, chachameinu,
avadecha z"l katevu: ayin
ro'ah veleiv chomeid uchelei
hamma'aseh gomerim. vechein:
ein appatroppos la'arayot.
Vegalui veyadua' lefanecha ki
yeitzer hara yesodo me'eish
va'ani basar vadam, ve'im ein
attah ozeir li, ein bi et hakkoach
lehitmoded kenegdo, lachein
yehi ratzon millefanecha adonai
eloheinu ve'elohei avoteinu
shettesayyei'a beyadi vetein bi
ratzon, chochmah, binah veda'at,
koach viyicholet shello atur achar
libbi velo achar einai, kedichtiv:
ha'aveir einai mere'ot shav
bidrachecha chayyeini. Vezakkeini
ligdor gederot le'atzmi be'ofen
shello em'ad, veyihyeh libbi

בְּרַחֲמִים עֲצוּמִים עַל גּוּפִי,
נַפְשִׁי, רוּחִי וְנִשְׁמָתִי וְהָסֵר
מִתּוֹכִי כָּל מִדּוֹת רָעוֹת וְכָל
נְטִיּוֹת שֶׁאֵינָן רְצוּיוֹת וְאַל
יִשְׁלְטוּ בִּי כֹּחוֹת הַטֻּמְאָה:
רְצֵה יְיָ לְהַצִּילֵנִי יְיָ
לְעֶזְרָתִי חוּשָׁה. וְהַצִּילֵנִי
יְיָ אֱלֹהַי מִמַּחְשָׁבוֹת
רָעוֹת וּמִכָּל חֵטְא עָוֹן וּפֶשַׁע
כְּדִכְתִיב: אַתָּה סֵתֶר לִי מִצַּר
תִּצְּרֵנִי רָנֵּי פַלֵּט תְּסוֹבְבֵנִי
סֶלָה.

רִבּוֹנוֹ שֶׁל עוֹלָם, חֲכָמֵנוּ,
עֲבָדֶךָ ז"ל כָּתְבוּ: עַיִן
רוֹאָה וְלֵב חוֹמֵד וּכְלֵי
הַמַּעֲשֶׂה גּוֹמְרִים: וְכֵן:
אֵין אַפַּטְרוֹפּוֹס לָעֲרָיוֹת.
וְגָלוּי וְיָדוּעַ לְפָנֶיךָ כִּי
יֵצֶר הָרָע יְסוֹדוֹ מֵאֵשׁ
וַאֲנִי בָּשָׂר וָדָם, וְאִם אֵין
אַתָּה עוֹזֵר לִי, אֵין בִּי אֶת הַכֹּחַ
לְהִתְמוֹדֵד כְּנֶגְדּוֹ לָכֵן
יְהִי רָצוֹן מִלְּפָנֶיךָ יְיָ
אֱלֹהֵינוּ וֵאלֹהֵי אֲבוֹתֵינוּ
שֶׁתְּסַיֵּעַ בְּיָדִי וְתֵן בִּי
רָצוֹן, חָכְמָה, בִּינָה וְדַעַת,
כֹּחַ וִיכֹלֶת שֶׁלֹּא אָתוּר אַחַר
לִבִּי וְלֹא אַחַר עֵינַי, כְּדִכְתִיב:
הַעֲבֵר עֵינַי מֵרְאוֹת שָׁוְא
בִּדְרָכֶךָ חַיֵּנִי. וְזַכֵּנִי
לִגְדֹּר גְּדֵרוֹת לְעַצְמִי בְּאֹפֶן
שֶׁלֹּא אֶמְעַד, וְיִהְיֶה לִבִּי

נָכוֹן וּמָסוּר בְּיָדִי: לֵב טָהוֹר
בְּרָא לִי אֱלֹהִים וְרוּחַ נָכוֹן
חַדֵּשׁ בְּקִרְבִּי: כִּי לְךָ יְיָ
הוֹחָלְתִּי אַתָּה תַעֲנֶה אֲדֹנָי
אֱלֹהָי. וּבָרְכֵנִי אָבִי וְהָסֵר
מִמֶּנִּי כָּל יָגוֹן וַאֲנָחָה,
וְהַאֲצֵל עָלַי אוֹר וְשִׂמְחָה
קְדֻשָּׁה וְטָהֳרָה, וְתַלְבִּשֵׁנִי
בְּרוּחַ טוֹבָה: וְרוּחַ נְדִיבָה
תִסְמְכֵנִי, וְקַיֵּם בִּי:
וְנָחָה עָלָיו רוּחַ יְיָ רוּחַ
חָכְמָה וּבִינָה רוּחַ עֵצָה
וּגְבוּרָה רוּחַ דַּעַת וְיִרְאַת
יְיָ. וְצַוֵּה לְמַלְאָכֶיךָ
הַקְּדוֹשִׁים וְהַטְּהוֹרִים
הַמְמֻנִּים עַל פְּתִיחַת הַלֵּב
שֶׁיִּפְתְּחוּ אֶת לִבִּי בְּתוֹרָתֶךָ
כְּדִכְתִיב: גַּל עֵינַי וְאַבִּיטָה
נִפְלָאוֹת מִתּוֹרָתֶךָ: כִּי יְיָ
יִתֵּן חָכְמָה מִפִּיו דַּעַת
וּתְבוּנָה: בָּרוּךְ אַתָּה יְיָ
לַמְּדֵנִי חֻקֶּיךָ. וּמַלֵּא
אֶת לִבִּי וְאֶת לְבַב כָּל עַמְּךָ
בֵּית יִשְׂרָאֵל בְּאַהֲבָתֶךָ
וְיִרְאָתֶךָ וּבְאַהֲבַת תּוֹרָתֶךָ
הַקְּדוֹשָׁה וּבְאַהֲבַת יִשְׂרָאֵל
עַמֶּךָ. וְתַגְדִּיל וְתַגְבִּיר
וְתַרְבֶּה אֶת גְּבוּל הַקְּדֻשָּׁה
בְּעַמֶּךָ בֵּית יִשְׂרָאֵל
וְתַטֶּה אֶת לִבִּי וְאֶל לְבַב כָּל
עַמֶּךָ בֵּית יִשְׂרָאֵל לָלֶכֶת
בְּדֶרֶךְ הַתּוֹרָה וְהַמִּצְווֹת,
הַקְּדוֹשָׁה וְהַטָּהֳרָה,

nachon umasur beyadi: lev tahor
bera li elohim veruach nachon
chaddeish bekirbi: ki lecha adonai
hochaleti attah ta'aneh adonai
elohai. Uvarecheini avi vehasseir
mimmenni kol yagon va'anachah,
veha'atzeil alai or vesimchah
kedushah vetaharah, utelab'sheini
beruach tovah: veruach nedivah
tismecheini, vekayyem bi:
Venachah alav ruach adonai ruach
chochmah uvinah ruach eitzah
ugevurah ruach da'at veyir'at
adonai. Vetzavveh lemal'achecha
hakkedoshim vehattehorim
hammemunnim al petichat halleiv
sheyyiftechu et libbi betoratecha
kedichtiv: gal einai ve'abbitah
nifla'ot mittoratecha: ki adonai
yittein chochmah mippiv da'at
utevunah: baruch attah adonai
lammedeini chukkecha. Umallei
et libbi ve'et levav kol ammecha
beit yisra'el be'ahavatecha
veyir'atecha uve'ahavat toratecha
hakkedoshah uve'ahavat yisra'eil
ammecha. Vetagdil vetagbir
vetarbeh et gevul hakkedushah
be'ammecha beit yisra'el
vetatteh et libbi ve'el levav kol
ammecha beit yisra'el lallechet
bederech hattorah vehammitzvot,
hakkedushah vehattohorah,

vekayyeim banu: va'ani zot beriti otam amar adonai, ruchi asher alecha udevarai asher samti beficha. Lo yamushu mippicha umippi zar'acha umippi zera zar'acha amar adonai mei'attah ve'ad olam: vechein: ki male'ah ha'aretz dei'ah et adonai kammayim layyam mechassim amein ken yehi ratzon netzach selah va'ed.

Uvetoratecha katuv leimor: shema yisra'el adonai eloheinu adonai echad.

Yehi adonai eloheinu immanu ka'asher hayah im avoteinu al ya'azveinu ve'al yittesheinu, lehattot levaveinu eilav. Lalechet bechol derachav velishmor mitzvotav vechukkav umishpatav, asher tzivvah et avoteinu: veyihyu devarai eilleh asher hitchannanti lifnei adonai, kerovim el adonai eloheinu yomam valai'lah. La'asot mishpat avdo umishpat ammo yisra'el devar yom beyomo: lema'an da'at kol ammei ha'aretz, ki adonai hu ha'elohim ein od:

eleicha adonai ekra ve'eil adonai etchannan: eretz natenah yevulah

וְקַיֵּם בָּנוּ: וַאֲנִי זֹאת בְּרִיתִי אוֹתָם אָמַר יְיָ, רוּחִי אֲשֶׁר עָלֶיךָ וּדְבָרַי אֲשֶׁר שַׂמְתִּי בְּפִיךָ. לֹא יָמוּשׁוּ מִפִּיךָ וּמִפִּי זַרְעֲךָ וּמִפִּי זֶרַע זַרְעֲךָ אָמַר יְיָ מֵעַתָּה וְעַד עוֹלָם: וְכֵן: כִּי מָלְאָה הָאָרֶץ דֵּעָה אֶת יְיָ כַּמַּיִם לַיָּם מְכַסִּים אָמֵן כֵּן יְהִי רָצוֹן נֶצַח סֶלָה וָעֶד.

וּבְתוֹרָתְךָ כָּתוּב לֵאמֹר: שְׁמַע יִשְׂרָאֵל יְיָ אֱלֹהֵינוּ יְיָ אֶחָד.

יְהִי יְיָ אֱלֹהֵינוּ עִמָּנוּ כַּאֲשֶׁר הָיָה עִם אֲבֹתֵינוּ אַל יַעַזְבֵנוּ וְאַל יִטְּשֵׁנוּ, לְהַטּוֹת לְבָבֵנוּ אֵלָיו. לָלֶכֶת בְּכָל דְּרָכָיו וְלִשְׁמֹר מִצְוֺתָיו וְחֻקָּיו וּמִשְׁפָּטָיו, אֲשֶׁר צִוָּה אֶת אֲבֹתֵינוּ: וְיִהְיוּ דְבָרַי אֵלֶּה אֲשֶׁר הִתְחַנַּנְתִּי לִפְנֵי יְיָ, קְרֹבִים אֶל יְיָ אֱלֹהֵינוּ יוֹמָם וָלָיְלָה. לַעֲשׂוֹת מִשְׁפַּט עַבְדוֹ וּמִשְׁפַּט עַמּוֹ יִשְׂרָאֵל דְּבַר יוֹם בְּיוֹמוֹ: לְמַעַן דַּעַת כָּל עַמֵּי הָאָרֶץ, כִּי יְיָ הוּא הָאֱלֹהִים אֵין עוֹד:

אֵלֶיךָ יְיָ אֶקְרָא וְאֶל אֲדֹנָי אֶתְחַנָּן: אֶרֶץ נָתְנָה יְבוּלָהּ

yevarecheinu elohim eloheinu:

יְבָרְכֵנוּ אֱלֹהִים אֱלֹהֵינוּ:

adonai tzeva'ot immanu misgav
lanu eilohei ya'akov selah, adonai
tzeva'ot ashrei adam botei'ach
bach, adonai hoshi'ah hammelech
ya'aneinu veyom kare'einu.

יְיָ צְבָאוֹת עִמָּנוּ מִשְׂגָּב
לָנוּ אֱלֹוהֵי יַעֲקֹב סֶלָה, יְיָ
צְבָאוֹת אַשְׁרֵי אָדָם בֹּטֵחַ
בָּךְ, יְיָ הוֹשִׁיעָה הַמֶּלֶךְ
יַעֲנֵנוּ בְיוֹם קָרְאֵנוּ.

Yihyu leratzon imrei fi, vehegyon
libbi lefanecha adonai tzuri
vego'ali.

יִהְיוּ לְרָצוֹן אִמְרֵי פִי, וְהֶגְיוֹן
לִבִּי לְפָנֶיךָ יְיָ צוּרִי
וְגֹאֲלִי.

Notes

_____

_____

_____

_____

_____

_____

_____

_____

_____

_____

_____

_____

Prayer to Serve God in the Present Moment

S ERVING GOD MIGHT seem overwhelming at first. Where do we begin? How can we achieve all that we aspire to within our limited time on Earth? The Psalmist offers a grounding perspective: "*Today*, if you listen to His voice" (Psalms 95:7). According to Rabbi Natan of Breslov (1780-1844), this teaches us the importance of living in the present, of focusing on serving God today rather than getting caught up in what tomorrow or next year might bring. This verse also encourages us not to delay our spiritual duties to a future that is uncertain.

The following is a prayer by Rabbi Natan of Breslov asking God for help to serve Him in the present moment:

"Come, let us bow down and prostrate ourselves; let us bow before the Lord our Maker. For He is our God and we are the nation of His pasture and the flock in His hand — today, if you listen to His voice."

Full of Mercy, Master of wonders, You Who every day renew the act of Creation in Your goodness, You Who in Your wisdom bring about the passage of time, help me renew myself every day in order to increase holiness and purity. Every day, may I begin anew to serve You as though I had been born today.

May I not think beyond today. May my mind never grow confused by thinking of the past or the future.

May the coming days and hours not concern me. May I not contemplate them, for that might hamper my ability to serve You. Instead, may I only consider the present day, hour and minute. As a result, may I serve You wholeheartedly, without any confusion, fear, heaviness or laziness.

Every day, may I enthusiastically serve You anew. May I place nothing before my eyes but this day, hour and minute, so that I will serve You energetically.

And let no matter of service that is truly Your will be difficult for me. May I deal with just one day at a time, for in one day one can endure all the labors of the world.

In addition, may I not clutter my mind with concerns about making a living or taking care of my many needs from one day to the next. Instead, may I trust in You Who provides us with all of our needs every day. May I be accustomed to say always, "Blessed is God; every day, He gives us abundance, the God of our salvation."

Rescue me from the influence of people who lack faith, who worry about what they will eat and how they will take care of their many needs tomorrow. May I trust in Your Name and rely on You Who have shepherded me from my beginning.

Send me an abundance of goodness, each day in its time. You are the good King Who does good for everyone every day. You support us and provide for us every day and every hour, without fail. Even when we reach old age and our hair turns white, You will not abandon us. You will never leave us alone.

You who are full of mercy, have compassion on me and grant me the ability to achieve all this. May no concerns about anything in the world upset me. May I enter the realm of Your holiness, approach You and renew myself every day for the good. Every day and at every moment, may I add more holiness, purity and awe to my life as I engage in acts of worship.

May I not cheat myself by delaying my service of You from one day to the next. Rather, may I always consider that I have nothing but the present day and moment. May I strive to fulfill the obligations of the day, to do all that is within my capacity and not procrastinate, so that I will not be ashamed.

Rescue me every day with a new and wondrous salvation, so that I will approach You and come ever closer to You, in accordance with Your beneficent will.

"Sing to Hashem, all the land; proclaim His salvation from day to day." "Sing to Hashem, bless His Name, proclaim His salvation from day to day."

From this moment onward, during the few days that I have at my disposal in this transient world, help me renew my days.

"Teach us to count our days, and then we will acquire a heart of wisdom. Return, Hashem; how long must we wait? Relent concerning Your servants. Satisfy us in the morning with Your kindness; may we sing and rejoice all of our days. Give us joy commensurate to the days that You afflicted us, the years that we saw evil."

"Return us to You, Hashem, and we will return; renew our days as of old." "Hashem, may Your kindness be upon us as we have hoped in You."

"May Hashem our God be with us as He was with our fathers. May He not abandon us and never leave us. May He incline our hearts to Him, so that we will walk in all of His ways and guard the commandments, rules and laws that He gave our fathers. May these words which I have pleaded before Hashem be close to Hashem our God day and night, so that He will act righteously on behalf of His servant and perform justice for His nation every day. Then may all of the nations of the land know that Hashem is God — there is no other!"

Bo'u nishtachaveh venichra'ah nivrechah lifnei adonai osenu. Ki hu eloheinu va'anachnu am mar'ito vetzon yado hayyom im bekolo tishma'u.

בֹּאוּ נִשְׁתַּחֲוֶה וְנִכְרָעָה נִבְרְכָה לִפְנֵי יְהֹוָה עוֹשֵׂנוּ. כִּי הוּא אֱלֹהֵינוּ וַאֲנַחְנוּ עַם מַרְעִיתוֹ וְצֹאן יָדוֹ הַיּוֹם אִם בְּקֹלוֹ תִשְׁמָעוּ.

Malei rachamim, adon hannifla'ot, hammechaddeish betuvo bechol yom tamid ma'aseih vereishit, asher bitvunatecha attah meshanneh ittim umachalif et hazzemannim, azereini vehoshi'eini bishu'atecha haggedolah vehannifla'ah, she'ezkeh lechaddeish et atzmi bechol yom betosefet kedushah vetohorah be'emet, she'ezkeh bechol yom lehatchil mechadash ba'avodatecha hakkedoshah ke'illu noladti hayyom, velo echshov miyyom lachavero kelal, velo yuchelu levalbel et da'ti kelal miyyom lachaveiro,

מָלֵא רַחֲמִים, אֲדוֹן הַנִּפְלָאוֹת, הַמְחַדֵּשׁ בְּטוּבוֹ בְּכָל יוֹם תָּמִיד מַעֲשֵׂה בְרֵאשִׁית, אֲשֶׁר בִּתְבוּנָתֶךָ אַתָּה מְשַׁנֶּה עִתִּים וּמַחֲלִיף אֶת הַזְּמַנִּים, עָזְרֵנִי וְהוֹשִׁיעֵנִי בִּישׁוּעָתְךָ הַגְּדוֹלָה וְהַנִּפְלָאָה, שֶׁאֶזְכֶּה לְחַדֵּשׁ אֶת עַצְמִי בְּכָל יוֹם בְּתוֹסֶפֶת קְדֻשָּׁה וְטָהֳרָה בֶּאֱמֶת, שֶׁאֶזְכֶּה בְּכָל יוֹם לְהַתְחִיל מֵחָדָשׁ בַּעֲבוֹדָתְךָ הַקְּדוֹשָׁה כְּאִלּוּ נוֹלַדְתִּי הַיּוֹם, וְלֹא אֶחְשֹׁב מִיּוֹם לַחֲבֵרוֹ כְּלָל, וְלֹא יוּכְלוּ לְבַלְבֵּל אֶת דַּעְתִּי כְּלָל מִיּוֹם לַחֲבֵרוֹ,

hein mehe'avar, hen meihe'atid,
Velo yachbidu alai et ha'avodah
al-yedei hayyamim habba'im
vehasha'ah ha'atidah, velo
estakkeil velo echshov beda'ti ki
im oto hayyom ve'otah hasha'ah
veharega she'ani omeid bah
az, be'ofen she'uchal la'asok
ba'avodatecha be'emet bitmimut
beli shum bilbulim ufechadim
ucheveidut ve'atzlut, rak
ezdareiz ba'avodatecha bechol
yom meichadash, velo asim
leneged einai ki im oto hayyom
vehasha'ah veharega levad,
lema'an etchazzeik al-yedei-zeh
ba'avodatecha be'emet

Velo yihyeh kaveid alai shum
devar avodah shehu retzonecha
be'emet, ki al yom echad yecholin
lisbol kol ha'avodot shebba'olam.

Vechein lo avalbeil et da'ti
befarnasati vehitztarchutai
hammerubbim miyyom lachaveiro
kelal, rak evtach badonai
be'emet asher hu mashpia'
lanu kol hitztarechuteinu bechol
yom vayom. Ve'ehyeh ragil
lomar bechol eit, baruch adonai
yom yom ya'amas lanu ha'eil
yeshu'ateinu selah.

הֵן מֵהֶעָבָר, הֵן מֵהֶעָתִיד,
וְלֹא יַכְבִּידוּ עָלַי אֶת הָעֲבוֹדָה
עַל־יְדֵי הַיָּמִים הַבָּאִים
וְהַשָּׁעָה הָעֲתִידָה, וְלֹא
אֶסְתַּכֵּל וְלֹא אֶחְשֹׁב בְּדַעְתִּי כִּי
אִם אוֹתוֹ הַיּוֹם וְאוֹתָהּ הַשָּׁעָה
וְהָרֶגַע שֶׁאֲנִי עוֹמֵד בָּהּ
אָז, בְּאֹפֶן שֶׁאוּכַל לַעֲסֹק
בַּעֲבוֹדָתְךָ בֶּאֱמֶת בִּתְמִימוּת
בְּלִי שׁוּם בִּלְבּוּלִים וּפְחָדִים
וּכְבֵדוּת וְעַצְלוּת, רַק
אֶזְדָּרֵז בַּעֲבוֹדָתְךָ בְּכָל
יוֹם מֵחָדָשׁ, וְלֹא אָשִׂים
לְנֶגֶד עֵינַי כִּי אִם אוֹתוֹ הַיּוֹם
וְהַשָּׁעָה וְהָרֶגַע לְבַד,
לְמַעַן אֶתְחַזֵּק עַל־יְדֵי־זֶה
בַּעֲבוֹדָתְךָ בֶּאֱמֶת.

וְלֹא יִהְיֶה כָּבֵד עָלַי שׁוּם
דְּבַר עֲבוֹדָה שֶׁהוּא רְצוֹנְךָ
בֶּאֱמֶת, כִּי עַל יוֹם אֶחָד
יְכוֹלִין לִסְבֹּל כָּל הָעֲבוֹדוֹת שֶׁבָּעוֹלָם,

וְכֵן לֹא אֲבַלְבֵּל אֶת דַּעְתִּי
בְּפַרְנָסָתִי וְהִצְטָרְכוּתַי
הַמְרֻבִּים מִיּוֹם לַחֲבֵרוֹ
כְּלָל, רַק אֶבְטַח בַּיהוָה
בֶּאֱמֶת אֲשֶׁר הוּא מַשְׁפִּיעַ לָנוּ
כָּל הִצְטָרְכוּתֵנוּ בְּכָל
יוֹם וָיוֹם. וְאֶהְיֶה רָגִיל
לוֹמַר בְּכָל־עֵת, בָּרוּךְ אֲדֹנָי
יוֹם יוֹם יַעֲמָס לָנוּ הָאֵל
יְשׁוּעָתֵנוּ סֶלָה.

Vetatzileinu mimmechusserei
amanah haddo'agim vechoshevim
mah yochlu lemachar,
umeiheichan yavo hitztarechutam
hammerubbeh lemachar,
rak evtach besheim adonai
ve'esha'en belohai. Ha'elohim
haro'eh oti me'odi hu yashpia'
li kol tov devar yom beyomo,
hammelech hattov vehammeitiv
lakkol bechol yom vayom, hu
heitiv hu meitiv hu yeitiv lanu
veefarneseinu veechalkeleinu
tamid bechol yom uvechol-eit
uvechol sha'ah be'ein machsor
davar, vegam ad ziknah veseivah
elohim al ya'azveinu ve'al
yittesheinu ad olam:

Malei rachamim, chamol alai
vezakkeni lavo lechol zeh, leval
tevalbeil oti hammachashavah
kelal miyyom lachaveiro beshum
davar shebba'olam, be'ofen
she'ezkeh lichnos bikdushatecha,
ulehitkarev eleicha be'emet,
ulehitchaddeish bechol yom
letovah, ulehosif bechol yom
uvechol-eit uvechol sha'ah tosefot
kedushah vetohorah veyir'at
adonai va'avodato be'emet.

Velo at'eh et atzmi velo edcheh

וְתַצִּילֵנוּ מִמַּחְסְרֵי
אֲמָנָה הַדּוֹאֲגִים וְחוֹשְׁבִים
מַה יֹּאכְלוּ לְמָחָר,
וּמֵהֵיכָן יָבוֹא הִצְטָרְכוּתָם
הַמְרֻבֶּה לְמָחָר,
רַק אֶבְטַח בְּשֵׁם יְהֹוָה
וְאֶשָּׁעֵן בֵּאלֹהָי. הָאֱלֹהִים
הָרוֹעֶה אוֹתִי מֵעוֹדִי הוּא יַשְׁפִּיעַ
לִי כָּל טוֹב דְּבַר יוֹם בְּיוֹמוֹ,
הַמֶּלֶךְ הַטּוֹב וְהַמֵּטִיב
לַכֹּל בְּכָל יוֹם וָיוֹם, הוּא
הֵטִיב הוּא מֵטִיב הוּא יֵיטִיב לָנוּ
וִיפַרְנְסֵנוּ וִיכַלְכְּלֵנוּ
תָּמִיד בְּכָל יוֹם וּבְכָל־עֵת
וּבְכָל שָׁעָה בְּאֵין מַחְסוֹר
דָּבָר, וְגַם עַד זִקְנָה וְשֵׂיבָה
אֱלֹהִים אַל יַעַזְבֵנוּ וְאַל
יִטְּשֵׁנוּ עַד עוֹלָם:

מָלֵא רַחֲמִים, חֲמֹל עָלַי
וְזַכֵּנִי לָבוֹא לְכָל זֶה, לְבַל
תְּבַלְבֵּל אוֹתִי הַמַּחֲשָׁבָה
כְּלָל מִיּוֹם לַחֲבֵרוֹ בְּשׁוּם
דָּבָר שֶׁבָּעוֹלָם, בְּאֹפֶן
שֶׁאֶזְכֶּה לִכְנֹס בִּקְדֻשָּׁתֶךָ,
וּלְהִתְקָרֵב אֵלֶיךָ בֶּאֱמֶת,
וּלְהִתְחַדֵּשׁ בְּכָל יוֹם
לְטוֹבָה, וּלְהוֹסִיף בְּכָל יוֹם
וּבְכָל־עֵת וּבְכָל שָׁעָה תּוֹסְפוֹת
קְדֻשָּׁה וְטָהֳרָה וְיִרְאַת
יְהֹוָה וַעֲבוֹדָתוֹ בֶּאֱמֶת.

וְלֹא אַטְעֶה אֶת עַצְמִי וְלֹא אֶדְחֶה

et ha'avodah miyyom lachaveiro
kelal, rak echshov bechol yom
ke'illu ein li be'olami ki im oto
hayyom ve'otah hasha'ah levad,
ve'eshtaddeil ve'et'ammeitz
bechol oz bechol yom latzeit
chovat hayyom, beyomo dayka,
kechol asher timtza yadi la'asot
bechochi be'oto hayyom ve'otah
hasha'ah dayka, velo eftor et
atzmi miyyom lachaveiro kelal,
lema'an lo eivosh velo ekkaleim
le'olam va'ed.

Azereini lema'an shemecha,
hoshi'eini bechol yom yeshu'ah
chadashah venifla'ah, be'ofen
she'ezkeh lehitkareiv eleicha
bechol yom behitkarevut
gadol yoter be'emet betachlit
hasheleimut kirtzonecha hattov,
vikuyyam mikra shekkatuv, shiru
ladonai kol ha'aretz basseru
miyyom el yom yeshu'ato.
Vene'emar, shiru ladonai barechu
shemo basseru miyyom leyom
yeshu'ato.

Zakkeini lehachayot et yamai
be'emet mei'attah al kol panim,
chamol al me'at yamai sheyyeish li
lehitmahmei'ah od bezeh ha'olam
ha'over, limnot yameinu kein hoda

אֶת הָעֲבוֹדָה מִיּוֹם לַחֲבֵרוֹ
כְּלָל, רַק אֶחְשֹׁב בְּכָל יוֹם
כְּאִלּוּ אֵין לִי בְּעוֹלָמִי כִּי אִם אוֹתוֹ
הַיּוֹם וְאוֹתָהּ הַשָּׁעָה לְבַד,
וְאֶשְׁתַּדֵּל וְאֶתְאַמֵּץ
בְּכָל עֹז בְּכָל יוֹם לָצֵאת
חוֹבַת הַיּוֹם, בְּיוֹמוֹ דַּיְקָא,
כְּכָל אֲשֶׁר תִּמְצָא יָדִי לַעֲשׂוֹת
בְּכֹחִי בְּאוֹתוֹ הַיּוֹם וְאוֹתָהּ
הַשָּׁעָה דַּיְקָא, וְלֹא אֶפְטֹר אֶת
עַצְמִי מִיּוֹם לַחֲבֵרוֹ כְּלָל,
לְמַעַן לֹא אֵבוֹשׁ וְלֹא אֶכָּלֵם
לְעוֹלָם וָעֶד.

עָזְרֵנִי לְמַעַן שְׁמֶךָ,
הוֹשִׁיעֵנִי בְּכָל יוֹם יְשׁוּעָה
חֲדָשָׁה וְנִכְלָאָה, בְּאֹפֶן
שֶׁאֶזְכֶּה לְהִתְקָרֵב אֵלֶיךָ
בְּכָל יוֹם בְּהִתְקָרְבוּת
גָּדוֹל יוֹתֵר בֶּאֱמֶת בְּתַכְלִית
הַשְּׁלֵמוּת כִּרְצוֹנְךָ הַטּוֹב,
וִיקֻיַּם מִקְרָא שֶׁכָּתוּב, שִׁירוּ
לַיהוָֹה כָּל הָאָרֶץ בַּשְּׂרוּ
מִיּוֹם אֶל יוֹם יְשׁוּעָתוֹ.
וְנֶאֱמַר, שִׁירוּ לַיהוָֹה בָּרְכוּ
שְׁמוֹ בַּשְּׂרוּ מִיּוֹם לְיוֹם
יְשׁוּעָתוֹ.

זַכֵּנִי לְהַחֲיוֹת אֶת יָמַי
בֶּאֱמֶת מֵעַתָּה עַל כָּל פָּנִים,
חֲמֹל עַל מְעַט יָמַי שֶׁיֵּשׁ לִי
לְהִתְמַהְמֵהַּ עוֹד בְּזֶה הָעוֹלָם
הָעוֹבֵר, לִמְנוֹת יָמֵינוּ כֵּן הוֹדַע

venavi levav chochmah. Shuvah
adonai ad matai vehinnachem al
avadecha. Sabbe'einu vabboker
chasdecha unerannenah
venismechah bechol yameinu,
sammecheinu kimot innitanu
shenot ra'inu ra'ah.
Hashiveinu adonai eleicha
venashuvah chaddeish yameinu
kekedem. Yehi chasdecha adonai
aleinu ka'asher yichalnu lach.

Yehi adonai eloheinu immanu
ka'asher hayah im avoteinu al
ya'azveinu ve'al yitteshinu.
Lehattot levaveinu eilav lalechet
bechol derachav velishmor
mitzvotav vechukkav umishpatav
asher tzivvah et avoteinu. Veyihyu
devarai elleh asher hitchannanti
lifnei adonai kerovim el adonai
eloheinu yomam valai'lah la'asot
mishpat avdo umishpat ammo
yisra'el devar yom beyomo.
Lema'an da'at kol ammei ha'aretz
ki adonai hu ha'elohim ein od:

וּנְבִיא לְבַב חָכְמָה. שׁוּבָה
יְהֹוָה עַד מָתָי וְהִנָּחֵם עַל
עֲבָדֶיךָ. שַׂבְּעֵנוּ בַבֹּקֶר
חַסְדֶּךָ וּנְרַנְּנָה
וְנִשְׂמְחָה בְּכָל יָמֵינוּ,
שַׂמְּחֵנוּ כִּימוֹת עִנִּיתָנוּ
שְׁנוֹת רָאִינוּ רָעָה.
הֲשִׁיבֵנוּ יְהֹוָה אֵלֶיךָ
וְנָשׁוּבָה חַדֵּשׁ יָמֵינוּ
כְּקֶדֶם. יְהִי חַסְדְּךָ יְהֹוָה
עָלֵינוּ כַּאֲשֶׁר יִחַלְנוּ לָךְ.

יְהִי יְהֹוָה אֱלֹהֵינוּ עִמָּנוּ
כַּאֲשֶׁר הָיָה עִם אֲבוֹתֵינוּ אַל
יַעַזְבֵנוּ וְאַל יִטְּשֵׁנוּ.
לְהַטּוֹת לְבָבֵנוּ אֵלָיו לָלֶכֶת
בְּכָל דְּרָכָיו וְלִשְׁמֹר
מִצְוֹתָיו וְחֻקָּיו וּמִשְׁפָּטָיו
אֲשֶׁר צִוָּה אֶת אֲבוֹתֵינוּ. וְיִהְיוּ
דְבָרַי אֵלֶּה אֲשֶׁר הִתְחַנַּנְתִּי
לִפְנֵי יְהֹוָה קְרֹבִים אֶל יְהֹוָה
אֱלֹהֵינוּ יוֹמָם וָלָיְלָה לַעֲשׂוֹת
מִשְׁפַּט עַבְדּוֹ וּמִשְׁפַּט עַמּוֹ
יִשְׂרָאֵל דְּבַר יוֹם בְּיוֹמוֹ.
לְמַעַן דַּעַת כָּל עַמֵּי הָאָרֶץ
כִּי יְהֹוָה הוּא הָאֱלֹהִים אֵין עוֹד:

Notes

Prayer for Oneself and One's Children to Return to God's Ways

IN THE FOLLOWING prayer, we ask God to remove any negative traits and desires hindering our spiritual growth and the spiritual growth of our children, reinforcing our commitment to better ourselves and draw closer to the Divine. Moreover, we seek His grace in guiding our children closer to His word, fostering a lifelong bond with Him and His teachings.

May it be Your will before You, Lord our God and God of our ancestors, that You remove from me all bad traits and all desires, and please fulfill in me the verse "and your Lord God will circumcise your heart and the heart of your offspring, to love the Lord your God with all your heart and with all your soul, that you may live." And remove from all our offspring all the obstacles that prevent them from engaging in the study of Your holy Bible, and bestow upon them the causes that will bring them to engage in Your holy Torah with joy and love. Blessed are You, Lord, who desires repentance.

Yehi ratzon millefanecha	יְהִי רָצוֹן מִלְפָנֶיךָ
adonai eloheinu velohei	יי אֱלֹהֵינוּ וֵאלֹהֵי
avoteinu shettasir mimmenni	אֲבוֹתֵינוּ שֶׁתָּסִיר מִמֶּנִּי
kol hammiddot hara'ot ve'et kol	כָּל הַמִּדּוֹת הָרָעוֹת וְאֶת כָּל
hatta'avot vekayyeim na bi "umal	הַתַּאֲווֹת וְקַיֶּם נָא בִּי "וּמָל
adonai elohecha et levavecha	יְהוָה אֱלֹהֶיךָ אֶת לְבָבְךָ

ve'et levav zar'echa le'ahavah	וְאֶת לְבַב זַרְעֶךָ לְאַהֲבָה
et adonai elohecha bechol	אֶת יְהֹוָה אֱלֹהֶיךָ בְּכָל
levavecha uvechol nafshecha	לְבָבְךָ וּבְכָל נַפְשֶׁךָ
lema'an chayyecha" vehaser	לְמַעַן חַיֶּיךָ״ וְהָסֵר
mizzar'einu et kol hassibbot	מִזַּרְעֵנוּ אֶת כָּל הַסִּבּוֹת
hammone'ot otam la'asok	הַמּוֹנְעוֹת אוֹתָם לַעֲסֹק
betoratecha hakkedoshah	בְּתוֹרָתְךָ הַקְּדוֹשָׁה
vetamshich aleihem et hassibbot	וְתַמְשִׁיךָ עֲלֵיהֶם אֶת הַסִּבּוֹת
sheyyavi'u otam la'asok	שֶׁיָּבִיאוּ אוֹתָם לַעֲסֹק
betoratecha hakkedoshah	בְּתוֹרָתְךָ הַקְּדוֹשָׁה
besimchah ve'ahavah, baruch	בְּשִׂמְחָה וְאַהֲבָה, בָּרוּךְ
attah adonai harotzeh bitshuvah	אַתָּה יי הָרוֹצֶה בִּתְשׁוּבָה

Notes

_____

_____

_____

_____

_____

_____

_____

_____

_____

_____

_____

_____

Psalm of Repentance

P SALM 51, AUTHORED by King David, was aptly termed the "Psalm of Repentance" by Rabbi Jonah Gerondi (1180-1263), author of a comprehensive work on repentance. Through vivid appeals like "wash me" and "purify me," David reveals repentance as a transformative gift from God, capable of altering reality and offering a fresh start. As long as we live, God eagerly awaits our acknowledgement of wrongdoing and our return to Him with love. Reciting this psalm is the first step towards embracing that transformative journey of repentance, inviting us to begin our own path back to God's open arms.

For the leader. A psalm of David, when Nathan the prophet came to him after he had come to Bathsheba. Have mercy upon me, O God, as befits Your faithfulness; in keeping with Your abundant compassion, blot out my transgressions. Wash me thoroughly of my iniquity, and purify me of my sin; for I recognize my transgressions, and am ever conscious of my sin. Against You alone have I sinned, and done what is evil in Your sight; so You are just in Your sentence, and right in Your judgment. Indeed I was born with iniquity; with sin my mother conceived me. Indeed You desire truth about that which is hidden; teach me wisdom about secret things. Purge me with hyssop till I am pure; wash me till I am whiter than snow. Let me hear tidings of joy and gladness; let the bones You have crushed exult. Hide Your face from my sins; blot out all my iniquities. Fashion a pure heart for me, O God; create in me a steadfast spirit. Do not cast me out of Your presence, or take Your holy spirit away from me. Let me again rejoice in Your help; let a vigorous spirit sustain me. I will teach transgressors Your ways, that sinners may return to You. Save me from bloodguilt, O God, God, my deliverer, that I may sing forth Your beneficence. O Lord, open my lips, and let my mouth declare Your praise. You do not want me to bring sacrifices; You do not desire burnt offerings; True sacrifice to God is a contrite spirit; God, You will not despise a contrite and crushed heart. May it please You to make Zion prosper; rebuild the walls of Jerusalem. Then You will want sacrifices offered in righteousness, burnt and whole offerings; then bulls will be offered on Your altar.

Lammenatzei'ach mizmor ledavid.	לַמְנַצֵּחַ מִזְמוֹר לְדָוִד:
Bevo eilav natan hannavi ka'asher	בְּבוֹא־אֵלָיו נָתָן הַנָּבִיא כַּאֲשֶׁר־
ba el batshava. Chonneini	בָּא אֶל־בַּת־שָׁבַע: חָנֵּנִי
elohim kechasdecha kerov	אֱלֹהִים כְּחַסְדֶּךָ כְּרֹב
rachamecha mecheih fesha'ai.	רַחֲמֶיךָ מְחֵה פְשָׁעָי:
herev kabbeseini mei'avoni	הֶרֶב כַּבְּסֵנִי מֵעֲוֹנִי
umechattati tahareini. Ki fesha'ai	וּמֵחַטָּאתִי טַהֲרֵנִי: כִּי־פְשָׁעַי
ani eida vechattati negdi tamid.	אֲנִי אֵדָע וְחַטָּאתִי נֶגְדִּי תָמִיד:
Lecha levaddecha chatati vehara	לְךָ לְבַדְּךָ חָטָאתִי וְהָרַע
be'einecha asiti lema'an titzdak	בְּעֵינֶיךָ עָשִׂיתִי לְמַעַן תִּצְדַּק
bedovrecha tizkeh veshoftecha.	בְּדָבְרֶךָ תִּזְכֶּה בְשָׁפְטֶךָ:
Hein be'avon cholalti uvecheit	הֵן־בְּעָווֹן חוֹלָלְתִּי וּבְחֵטְא
yechematni immi. Hein emet	יֶחֱמַתְנִי אִמִּי: הֵן־אֱמֶת
chafatzta vattuchot uvesatum	חָפַצְתָּ בַטֻּחוֹת וּבְסָתֻם
chochmah todi'eini. Techatte'eini	חָכְמָה תוֹדִיעֵנִי: תְּחַטְּאֵנִי
ve'eizov v'et'har techabbeseini	בְאֵזוֹב וְאֶטְהָר תְּכַבְּסֵנִי
umisheleg albin. Tashmi'eini	וּמִשֶּׁלֶג אַלְבִּין: תַּשְׁמִיעֵנִי
sason vesimchah tageilnah	שָׂשׂוֹן וְשִׂמְחָה תָּגֵלְנָה
atzamot dikkita. Hasteir panecha	עֲצָמוֹת דִּכִּיתָ: הַסְתֵּר
meichata'i vechol avonotai	פָּנֶיךָ מֵחֲטָאָי וְכָל־
mecheih. Leiv tahor bera li elohim	עֲוֹנֹתַי מְחֵה: לֵב טָהוֹר
veruach nachon chaddeish	בְּרָא־לִי אֱלֹהִים וְרוּחַ נָכוֹן
bekirbi. Al tashlicheini	חַדֵּשׁ בְּקִרְבִּי: אַל־תַּשְׁלִיכֵנִי

millefanecha veruach kodshecha al tikkach mimmenni. Hashivah li seson yish'echa veruach nedivah tismecheini. Alammedah foshe'im derachecha vechatta'im eilecha yashuvu. Hatzileini middamim elohim elohei teshu'ati terannein leshoni tzidkatecha. Adonai sefatai tiftach ufi yaggid tehillatecha. Ki lo tachpotz zevach ve'etteinah olah lo tirtzeh. Zivchei elohim ruach nishbarah leiv nishbar venidkeh elohim lo tivzeh. Heitivah virtzon'cha et tziyyon tivneh chomot yerushalayim. Az tachpotz zivchei tzedek olah vechalil az ya'alu al mizbachacha farim.

מִלְּפָנֶיךָ וְרוּחַ קָדְשְׁךָ
אַל־תִּקַּח מִמֶּנִּי: הָשִׁיבָה
לִּי שְׂשׂוֹן יִשְׁעֶךָ וְרוּחַ
נְדִיבָה תִסְמְכֵנִי: אֲלַמְּדָה
כֹּשְׁעִים דְּרָכֶיךָ וְחַטָּאִים
אֵלֶיךָ יָשׁוּבוּ: הַצִּילֵנִי
מִדָּמִים אֱלֹהִים אֱלֹהֵי תְשׁוּעָתִי
תְּרַנֵּן לְשׁוֹנִי צִדְקָתֶךָ:
אֲדֹנָי שְׂפָתַי תִּפְתָּח וּפִי יַגִּיד
תְּהִלָּתֶךָ: כִּי לֹא־תַחְפֹּץ זֶבַח
וְאֶתֵּנָה עוֹלָה לֹא תִרְצֶה: זִבְחֵי
אֱלֹהִים רוּחַ נִשְׁבָּרָה לֵב־
נִשְׁבָּר וְנִדְכֶּה אֱלֹהִים לֹא תִבְזֶה:
הֵיטִיבָה בִרְצוֹנְךָ אֶת־צִיּוֹן
תִּבְנֶה חוֹמוֹת יְרוּשָׁלָםִ: אָז
תַּחְפֹּץ זִבְחֵי־צֶדֶק עוֹלָה
וְכָלִיל אָז יַעֲלוּ עַל־מִזְבַּחֲךָ
פָרִים:

Notes

_____

_____

_____

_____

_____

_____

_____

_____

Prayer of Confession

I N THE *VIDUY*, or Confession prayer, we openly acknowledge our sins before God and seek forgiveness. This prayer highlights a profound truth: the true value of our lives is not measured by material success or achievements, but by the depth of our relationships with God and those around us. Recited on the Day of Atonement and at life's end, yet appropriate at any time of the year, the *Viduy* resonates deeply, calling for introspection and spiritual growth.

When reciting *Viduy* we stand humbly, our bodies bowed, as we acknowledge and confess each sin. With every confession, we express deep regret and firmly resolve to turn away from these missteps. Through this act, we seek to shed the burdens of past transgressions, embarking on a path of spiritual purification and renewal.

Our God and God of our fathers, let our prayer come before you and do not ignore our supplication. For we are not so brazen-faced and stiff-necked to say to you, Lord, our God, and God of our fathers, We are righteous and have not sinned. But, indeed, we and our fathers have sinned.

We have trespassed against God and man, and we are devastated by our guilt; We have betrayed God and man, we have been ungrateful for the good done to us; We have stolen; We have slandered. We have caused others to sin; We have caused others to commit sins for which they are called wicked; We have sinned with malicious intent; We have forcibly taken other's possessions even though we paid for them; We have added falsehood upon falsehood; we have joined with evil individuals or groups. We have given harmful advice; We have deceived; We have mocked; We have rebelled against God and His Bible; We have caused God to be angry with us; We have turned away from God's Bible; We have sinned deliberately; We have been negligent in our performance of the commandments; We have caused our friends grief; We have been stiff-necked, refusing to admit that the cause of our suffering is our own sins. We have committed sins for which we are called evil, such as raising a hand to hit someone. We have committed sins which are the result of moral corruption; We have committed sins which the Bible refers to as abominations; We have gone astray; We have led others astray.

We have turned away from Your commandments and from Your good laws, and we have gained nothing from it. And You are the Righteous One in all punishment that has come upon us; for You have acted truthfully and we have acted wickedly.

You are Almighty, slow to anger, Lord of Mercy You are called, and the way of repentance You have taught us. The greatness of Your mercy and kindness, remember this day and every day for the descendants of Your loved ones. Turn to us with compassion for You are the Lord of Mercy. With supplication and prayer we approach Your Presence, as You made known to Moses, the modest one of old. From Your fierce anger turn, as it is written in Your Bible: In the shadow of Your wings, may we be sheltered and lodged, as on the day of which it is said: When the Lord descended in the cloud. Remove our transgression, and blot out our iniquity, as on the day of which it is said: And He stood with him there. Give ear to our cry and listen to our speech, as on the day of which it is said: And He proclaimed in the Name, Lord, and there it is said:

And the Lord passed before Moses and proclaimed:

Lord, Lord, Almighty, Merciful, Gracious, Slow to Anger, and Abundant in Kindness and Truth. Keeper of kindness for thousands of generations, Endurer of iniquity and transgression, and sin, and Acquitter of those who repent.

And pardon our iniquity and our sin, and take us for Your inheritance. Pardon us, our Father, for we have sinned, forgive us, our King, for we have transgressed. For You, my Master, are good and forgiving, and abounding in kindness to all who call upon You.

Eloheinu veilohei avoteinu	אֱלֹהֵינוּ וֵאלֹהֵי אֲבוֹתֵינוּ
tavo lefanecha tefillateinu, ve'al	תָּבֹא לְפָנֶיךָ תְּפִלָּתֵנוּ, וְאַל־
tit'allam mittechinnateinu she'ein	תִּתְעַלַּם מִתְּחִנָּתֵנוּ שֶׁאֵין
anu azzei fanim ukeshei oref	אָנוּ עַזֵּי פָנִים וּקְשֵׁי עֹרֶף
lomar lefanecha adonai eloheinu	לוֹמַר לְפָנֶיךָ יְהֹוָה אֱלֹהֵינוּ
veilohei avoteinu tzaddikim	וֵאלֹהֵי אֲבוֹתֵינוּ צַדִּיקִים
anachnu velo chatanu aval	אֲנַחְנוּ וְלֹא חָטָאנוּ אֲבָל
anachnu va'avoteinu chatanu:	אֲנַחְנוּ וַאֲבוֹתֵינוּ חָטָאנוּ׃

Ashamnu. Bagadnu. Gazalnu.	אָשַׁמְנוּ. בָּגַדְנוּ. גָּזַלְנוּ.
Dibbarnu dofi. He'evinu.	דִּבַּרְנוּ דֹּפִי. הֶעֱוִינוּ.
Vehirsha'nu. zadnu. Chamasnu.	וְהִרְשַׁעְנוּ. זַדְנוּ. חָמַסְנוּ.
Tafalnu sheker. Ya'atznu ra.	טָפַלְנוּ שֶׁקֶר. יָעַצְנוּ רָע.
Kizzavnu. latznu. Maradnu.	כִּזַּבְנוּ. לַצְנוּ. מָרַדְנוּ.
Ni'atznu. Sararnu. Avinu. Pasha'nu.	נִאַצְנוּ. סָרַרְנוּ. עָוִינוּ. פָּשַׁעְנוּ.
Tzararnu. Kishinu oref. Rasha'nu.	צָרַרְנוּ. קִשִּׁינוּ עֹרֶף. רָשַׁעְנוּ.
Shichatnu. Ti'avnu. Ta'inu.	שִׁחַתְנוּ. תִּעַבְנוּ. תָּעִינוּ.
Ti'ta'enu:	תִּעְתָּעְנוּ׃

Sarnu mimmitzvotecha	סַרְנוּ מִמִּצְוֹתֶיךָ
umimmishpatecha hattovim velo	וּמִמִּשְׁפָּטֶיךָ הַטּוֹבִים וְלֹא
shavah lanu. Ve'attah tzaddik al	שָׁוָה לָנוּ. וְאַתָּה צַדִּיק עַל
kol habba aleinu. Ki emet asita	כָּל הַבָּא עָלֵינוּ. כִּי אֱמֶת עָשִׂיתָ

va'anachnu hirsha'enu:

וַאֲנַחְנוּ הִרְשָׁעְנוּ:

El erech appayim attah. Uva'al harachamim nikreita. Vederech teshuvah horeita: gedullat rachamecha vachasadecha. Tizkor hayyom uvechol yom lezera yedidecha: teifen eileinu berachamim. Ki attah hu ba'al harachamim: betachanun uvitfillah panecha nekaddeim. Kehoda'ta le'anav mikkedem: mecharon appecha shuv. Kemo betorat'cha katuv: uvetzeil kenafecha necheseh venitlonan. Keyom vayeired adonai be'anan: ta'avor al pesha vetimcheh asham. Keyom vaayyityatzeiv immo sham: ta'azin shav'ateinu vetakshiv menu ma'amar. Keyom vayyikra vesheim adonai, vesham ne'emar:

אֵל אֶרֶךְ־אַפַּיִם אַתָּה. וּבַעַל הָרַחֲמִים נִקְרֵאתָ. וְדֶרֶךְ תְּשׁוּבָה הוֹרֵיתָ: גְּדֻלַּת רַחֲמֶיךָ וַחֲסָדֶיךָ. תִּזְכֹּר הַיּוֹם וּבְכָל־יוֹם לְזֶרַע יְדִידֶיךָ: תֵּפֶן אֵלֵינוּ בְּרַחֲמִים. כִּי אַתָּה הוּא בַּעַל הָרַחֲמִים: בְּתַחֲנוּן וּבִתְפִלָּה פָּנֶיךָ נְקַדֵּם. כְּהוֹדַעְתָּ לֶעָנָו מִקֶּדֶם: מֵחֲרוֹן אַפְּךָ שׁוּב. כְּמוֹ בְּתוֹרָתְךָ כָּתוּב: וּבְצֵל כְּנָפֶיךָ נֶחֱסֶה וְנִתְלוֹנָן. כְּיוֹם וַיֵּרֶד יְהֹוָה בֶּעָנָן: תַּעֲבֹר עַל־פֶּשַׁע וְתִמְחֶה אָשָׁם. כְּיוֹם וַיִּתְיַצֵּב עִמּוֹ שָׁם: תַּאֲזִין שַׁוְעָתֵנוּ וְתַקְשִׁיב מֶנּוּ מַאֲמָר. כְּיוֹם וַיִּקְרָא בְשֵׁם יְהֹוָה, וְשָׁם נֶאֱמַר:

Vayya'avor adonai al panav vayyikra:

וַיַּעֲבֹר יְהֹוָה עַל פָּנָיו וַיִּקְרָא:

Adonai adonai el rachum vechannun erech appayim verav chesed ve'emet: notzeir chesed la'alafim nosei avon vafesha vechatta'ah venakkeh:

יְהֹוָה יְהֹוָה אֵל רַחוּם וְחַנּוּן אֶרֶךְ אַפַּיִם וְרַב־ חֶסֶד וֶאֱמֶת: נֹצֵר חֶסֶד לָאֲלָפִים נֹשֵׂא עָוֹן וָפֶשַׁע וְחַטָּאָה וְנַקֵּה:

Vesalachta la'avoneinu ulechattateinu unechaltanu:

וְסָלַחְתָּ לַעֲוֹנֵנוּ וּלְחַטָּאתֵנוּ וּנְחַלְתָּנוּ:

selach lanu avinu ki chatanu.
Mechal lanu malkeinu ki fasha'nu:
ki attah adonai tov vesallach verav
chesed lechol kore'echa:

סְלַח־לָֽנוּ אָבִֽינוּ כִּי־חָטָֽאנוּ.
מְחַל־לָֽנוּ מַלְכֵּֽנוּ כִּי־פָשָֽׁעְנוּ:
כִּי־אַתָּה אֲדֹנָי טוֹב וְסַלָּח וְרַב־
חֶֽסֶד לְכָל־קֹרְאֶֽיךָ:

Notes

_____

_____

_____

_____

_____

_____

_____

_____

_____

_____

_____

_____

_____

_____

_____

_____

_____

_____

Prayers of Praise and Thanks

THE PRAYERS IN this section open our hearts to the endless reasons for gratitude and praise. From the everyday miracles that sustain us, to the profound moments of deliverance and joy, and even the challenging times of our lives, these prayers guide us in expressing our deepest thanks to God. They help us recognize His presence in all aspects of our lives, celebrating His eternal kindness and love.

Psalm of Thanks

PSALM 100 IS a psalm of thanksgiving, calling on us to praise and thank God for His eternal love and kindness. While it is easy to see God's love and kindness in the good in our lives, it is more challenging to appreciate the lessons and growth opportunities within our struggles, and recognize that they, too, come from above. For them, as well, we must praise and thank God.

A psalm for praise. Raise a shout for the Lord, all the earth; worship the Lord in gladness; come into His presence with shouts of joy. Acknowledge that the Lord is God; He made us and we are His, His people, the flock He tends. Enter His gates with praise, His courts with acclamation. Praise Him! Bless His name! For the Lord is good; His steadfast love is eternal; His faithfulness is for all generations.

Mizmor letodah hari'u ladonai	מִזְמוֹר לְתוֹדָה הָרִיעוּ לַיהֹוָה
kol-ha'aretz. Ivdu et-adonai	כָּל־הָאָרֶץ: עִבְדוּ אֶת־יְהֹוָה
besimchah bo'u lefanav birnanah.	בְּשִׂמְחָה בֹּאוּ לְפָנָיו בִּרְנָנָה:
De'u ki-adonai hu elohim hu	דְּעוּ כִּי־יְהֹוָה הוּא אֱלֹהִים הוּא־
asanu velo anachnu ammo vetzon	עָשָׂנוּ וְלוֹ אֲנַחְנוּ עַמּוֹ וְצֹאן
mar'ito. bo'u she'arav betodah	מַרְעִיתוֹ: בֹּאוּ שְׁעָרָיו בְּתוֹדָה
chatzeirotav bit'hillah hodu lo	חֲצֵרֹתָיו בִּתְהִלָּה הוֹדוּ־לוֹ
barechu shemo. Ki tov adonai	בָּרְכוּ שְׁמוֹ: כִּי־טוֹב יְהֹוָה
le'olam chasdo ve'ad dor vador	לְעוֹלָם חַסְדּוֹ וְעַד־דֹּר וָדֹר
emunato.	אֱמוּנָתוֹ:

Psalm of Praise

PSALM 113 CALLS on everyone to praise God and His name. In our lives, we praise those who we appreciate. For those who serve God, the natural outgrowth is to praise the Lord from sunrise to sunset.

Halleluyah! Praise, servants of the Lord, praise the name of the Lord. May the Name of the Lord be blessed from now and forever. From the rising of the sun in the East to its setting, the name of the Lord is praised. Above all nations is the Lord, His honor is above the heavens. Who is like the Lord, our God, Who sits on high; Who looks down upon the heavens and the earth? He brings up the poor out of the dirt; from the refuse piles, He raises the destitute. To seat him with the nobles, with the nobles of his people. He sets the barren woman among her household as a happy mother of children. Halleluyah!

Haleluyah halelu avdei adonai halelu et sheim adonai: yehi sheim adonai mevorach mei'attah ve'ad olam: mimmizrach shemesh ad mevo'o mehullal sheim adonai: ram al kol goyim adonai al hashamayim kevodo: mi kadonai eloheinu hammagbihi lashavet: hammashpili lir'ot bashamayim uva'aretz: mekimi mei'afar dal mei'ashpot yarim evyon: lehoshivi im nedivim im nedivei ammo: moshivi akeret habbayit eim habbanim semeichah haleluyah:

הַלְלוּיָהּ הַלְלוּ עַבְדֵי יְהֹוָה הַלְלוּ אֶת שֵׁם יְהֹוָה: יְהִי שֵׁם יְהֹוָה מְבֹרָךְ מֵעַתָּה וְעַד־ עוֹלָם: מִמִּזְרַח־שֶׁמֶשׁ עַד־ מְבוֹאוֹ מְהֻלָּל שֵׁם יְהֹוָה: רָם עַל־כָּל־גּוֹיִם יְהֹוָה עַל הַשָּׁמַיִם כְּבוֹדוֹ: מִי כַּיהֹוָה אֱלֹהֵינוּ הַמַּגְבִּיהִי לָשָׁבֶת: הַמַּשְׁפִּילִי לִרְאוֹת בַּשָּׁמַיִם וּבָאָרֶץ: מְקִימִי מֵעָפָר דָּל מֵאַשְׁפֹּת יָרִים אֶבְיוֹן: לְהוֹשִׁיבִי עִם־נְדִיבִים עִם נְדִיבֵי עַמּוֹ: מוֹשִׁיבִי עֲקֶרֶת הַבַּיִת אֵם־ הַבָּנִים שְׂמֵחָה הַלְלוּיָהּ:

Prayer Upon Awakening in the Morning

MODEH ANI, WHICH means "I give thanks," is a Jewish prayer recited daily upon waking up in the morning. We thank God for restoring our souls each and every day.

I give thanks to You living and everlasting King for You have restored my soul with mercy. Great is Your faithfulness.

Modeh ani lefanecha melech
chai vekayyam shehechezarta
bi nishmati bechemlah, rabbah
emunatecha:

מוֹדֶה אֲנִי לְפָנֶיךָ מֶלֶךְ
חַי וְקַיָּם שֶׁהֶחֱזַרְתָּ
בִּי נִשְׁמָתִי בְּחֶמְלָה, רַבָּה
אֱמוּנָתֶךָ:

Notes

_____

_____

_____

_____

_____

_____

_____

_____

_____

Blessing After Using the Bathroom

THIS BLESSING, RECITED after using the bathroom, expresses deep gratitude for the intricate and precise functioning of the human body, designed with divine wisdom. It acknowledges the delicate balance necessary for life, recognizing that our very existence and ability to stand before the Creator depend on the perfect operation of our bodily systems. Through this blessing, we praise God, the healer of all flesh, who performs wonders every day in the most basic and essential aspects of our lives.

Blessed are You, Adonoy our God, King of the Universe, Who formed man with wisdom and created within him many openings and hollows. It is obvious and known in the presence of Your glorious throne that if one of them were ruptured, or if one of them were blocked, it would be impossible to exist and stand in Your Presence even for a short while. Blessed are You, Adonoy, Who heals all flesh and performs wonders.

Baruch attah adonai eloheinu	בָּרוּךְ אַתָּה ה׳ אֱלֹהֵינוּ
melech ha'olam asher yatzar	מֶלֶךְ הָעוֹלָם אֲשֶׁר יָצַר
et ha'adam bechochmah uvara	אֶת הָאָדָם בְּחָכְמָה וּבָרָא
vo nekavim nekavim chalulim	בוֹ נְקָבִים נְקָבִים חֲלוּלִים
chalulim. Galui veyadua' lifnei	חֲלוּלִים. גָּלוּי וְיָדוּעַ לִפְנֵי
chissei chevodecha she'im	כִּסֵּא כְבוֹדֶךָ שֶׁאִם
yippatei'ach echad meihem o	יִפָּתֵחַ אֶחָד מֵהֶם אוֹ
yissateim echad meihem i efshar	יִסָּתֵם אֶחָד מֵהֶם אִי אֶפְשָׁר
lehitkayyeim vela'amod lefanecha	לְהִתְקַיֵּם וְלַעֲמוֹד לְפָנֶיךָ

afilu sha'ah echat: baruch attah
adonai rofei chol basar umafli
la'asot:

אֲפִילוּ שָׁעָה אֶחָת: בָּרוּךְ אַתָּה
ה׳ רוֹפֵא כָל בָּשָׂר וּמַפְלִיא
לַעֲשׂוֹת:

Notes

Blessing of Thanks for Being Saved from a Dangerous Situation

THE *BIRKAT HAGOMEL*, the Blessing of Thanksgiving, is an expression of gratitude by those who have survived situations in which their lives were significantly at risk. This blessing is specifically recited by individuals who fall into one of four categories: those who have survived an overseas journey, navigated through a desert, recovered from severe illness, or been released from imprisonment. Additionally, it includes anyone who has been saved from other life-threatening circumstances such as surviving an accident or escaping from a natural disaster. The Thanksgiving Blessing is a recognition of the kindness and protection that God extends to us, thanking Him for the divine intervention that allowed us to overcome these perilous challenges.

Blessed are You, Lord our God, King of the Universe, Who bestows goodness upon the guilty, Who has bestowed every goodness upon me.

The congregation responds: *He Who has bestowed goodness upon you, may He bestow every goodness upon you, forever.*

Baruch attah adonai eloheinu	בָּרוּךְ אַתָּה ה׳ אֱלֹהֵינוּ
melech haolam, haggomeil	מֶלֶךְ הָעוֹלָם, הַגּוֹמֵל
lechayyavim tovot sheggemalani	לְחַיָּבִים טוֹבוֹת שֶׁגְּמָלַנִי
kol tov	כָּל טוֹב

Amen. Mi sheggemalecha tov. Hu
yigmalecha kol tov selah

אָמֵן. מִי שֶׁגְּמָלְךָ טוֹב. הוּא
יִגְמָלְךָ כָּל טוֹב סֶלָה

Notes

Prayer of Thanks to God for Everything

T HIS PRAYER IS an expression of gratitude directed towards the Almighty, acknowledging His never-ending kindness and the multitude of blessings He bestows upon us. Through this prayer, we recognize the divine hand in every aspect of our lives, the ones we perceive as positive as well as the ones we perceive as negative, and we thank God for them all.

King of Kings, Master of the Universe, Sovereign of the world,

Thank you!

Thank you for the fact that I am standing before You and giving thanks to You.

And everything that I say will be as nothing and void compared to how much I truly need to thank You. Indeed, for everything, I need to thank You.

Because everything is from You, You have given me everything with grace, kindness, and mercy.

Thank you for all the things in the world.

Thank you for the countless times You have helped me, supported me, saved me, delivered me, made me happy, healed me, protected me, cherished me.

Thank you for always being with me.

Thank you for giving me the strength to perform commandments, the strength to do good deeds, the strength to pray.

Thank you for all the times You helped and I didn't know to say thank you.

Thank you for the kindnesses You do for me at every moment.

Thank you for every breath I take.

Thank you, King of Kings, even for all the things I don't have, thank you for the times it's hard for me, thank you for the times I'm a bit sad, because everything is for my good, and even if I didn't always see that it is for my good, deep in my heart I know that everything that comes from You, Father, Master of the Universe, is good for me, and is done especially for me, with precise and perfect Divine Providence, as only the King of Kings can do.

Thank you for the fact that sometimes it's hard for me, because only then do I know to appreciate the good. Only after being in the dark, can one appreciate the light.

Thank you for the wonderful life You have given me.

Thank you for even the smallest thing I have, because You gave me everything, and no one else.

Thank you that You always hear my prayers, and the prayers of the people of Israel.

Creator of the Universe, I ask You for forgiveness from the depths of my heart if there were times I didn't appreciate what You gave me and instead of saying thank you, I only complained. Please never distance Yourself from me forever, I am but dust and ashes, and You are the entire world.

Melech malchei hammelachim,
adon olam, ribbono shel olam.

מֶלֶךְ מַלְכֵי הַמְּלָכִים,
אֲדוֹן עוֹלָם, רִבּוֹנוֹ שֶׁל עוֹלָם.

Todah!

תּוֹדָה!

Todah, she'ani omeid/omedet kan
lefanecha umodeh lecha.

תּוֹדָה, שֶׁאֲנִי עוֹמֵד/ת כָּאן
לְפָנֶיךָ וּמוֹדֶה לְךָ.

Vechol mah she'omer yihyeh
ke'ayin uche'efes le'ummat
kammah she'ani be'emet tzarich/
tzerichah lehodot lecha. Harei
al hakkol ani tzerch/tzerichah
lehodot lecha.

וְכָל מָה שֶׁאוֹמַר יִהְיֶה
כְּאַין וּכְאֶפֶס לְעֻמַּת
כַּמָּה שֶׁאֲנִי בֶּאֱמֶת צְרִיכ/ה
לְהוֹדוֹת לְךָ. הֲרֵי
עַל הַכֹּל אֲנִי צְרִיכ/ה
לְהוֹדוֹת לְךָ.

Ki hakkol mimmecha, hakkol
natatta li bechein, bechesed
uvarachamim.

כִּי הַכֹּל מִמְּךָ, הַכֹּל
נָתַתָּ לִי בְּחֵן, בְּחֶסֶד
וּבְרַחֲמִים.

Todah, al kol haddevarim ba'olam.

תּוֹדָה, עַל כָּל הַדְּבָרִים בָּעוֹלָם.

Todah, al rov rivei rivvot pe'amim
she'azarta li, tamachta bi, hosha'ta
oti, hitzalta oti, simmachta oti,
rippeita oti, shamarta alai, odad'ta
oti.

תּוֹדָה, עַל רֹב רִבֵּי רְבָבוֹת פְּעָמִים
שֶׁעֲזַרְתָּ לִי, תָּמַכְתָּ בִּי, הוֹשַׁעְתָּ
אוֹתִי, הִצַּלְתָּ אוֹתִי, שִׂמַּחְתָּ אוֹתִי,
רִפֵּאתָ אוֹתִי, שָׁמַרְתָּ עָלַי, עוֹדַדְתָּ
אוֹתִי.

Todah, she'attah itti tamid.

תּוֹדָה, שֶׁאַתָּה אִתִּי תָּמִיד.

Todah, she'attah notein li koach
la'asot mitzvot, koach la'asot
ma'asim tovim, koach lehitpalleil.

תּוֹדָה, שֶׁאַתָּה נוֹתֵן לִי כּוֹחַ
לַעֲשׂוֹת מִצְווֹת, כּוֹחַ לַעֲשׂוֹת
מַעֲשִׂים טוֹבִים, כּוֹחַ לְהִתְפַּלֵּל.

Todah, al kol happe'amim
she'azarta velo yada'ti lehaggid
todah.

תּוֹדָה, עַל כָּל הַפְּעָמִים
שֶׁעָזַרְתָּ וְלֹא יָדַעְתִּי לְהַגִּיד
תּוֹדָה.

Todah, al hachasadim she'attah
oseh immi, bechol rega verega.

תּוֹדָה, עַל הַחֲסָדִים שֶׁאַתָּה
עוֹשֶׂה עִמִּי, בְּכָל רֶגַע וְרֶגַע.

Todah, al kol neshimah uneshimah
she'ani noshem/noshemet.

תּוֹדָה, עַל כָּל נְשִׁימָה וּנְשִׁימָה
שֶׁאֲנִי נוֹשֵׁם/ת.

Todah, lecha melech malchei
hammelachim, gam al kol
haddevarim she'ein li, todah
shekkasheh li lif'amim, todah
shekketzat atzuv li lif'amim, ki
hakkol letovati, va'afillu im lo tamid
ra'iti shezzeh letovati, amok balleiv
ani yodea'/yoda'at shekkol mah
shemmaggia' mimmecha abba
ribbon olam - hu haddavar hattov
avuri, vehu na'asah bim'yuchad
bishvili, behashgachah peratit
meduyyeket umushlemet,
kemo sherak melech malchei
hammelachim yachol
la'asot.

תּוֹדָה, לְךָ מֶלֶךְ מַלְכֵי
הַמְּלָכִים, גַּם עַל כָּל
הַדְּבָרִים שֶׁאֵין לִי, תּוֹדָה
שֶׁקָּשֶׁה לִי לִפְעָמִים, תּוֹדָה
שֶׁקְּצָת עָצוּב לִי לִפְעָמִים, כִּי
הַכֹּל לְטוֹבָתִי, וַאֲפִלּוּ אִם לֹא תָּמִיד
רָאִיתִי שֶׁזֶּה לְטוֹבָתִי, עָמֹק בַּלֵּב
אֲנִי יוֹדֵעַ/ת שֶׁכָּל מָה
שֶׁמַּגִּיעַ מִמְּךָ אַבָּא
רִבּוֹן עוֹלָם - הוּא הַדָּבָר הַטּוֹב
עֲבוּרִי, וְהוּא נַעֲשָׂה בִּמְיֻחָד
בִּשְׁבִילִי, בְּהַשְׁגָּחָה פְּרָטִית
מְדֻיֶּקֶת וּמֻשְׁלֶמֶת,
כְּמוֹ שֶׁרַק מֶלֶךְ מַלְכֵי
הַמְּלָכִים יָכוֹל
לַעֲשׂוֹת.

Todah, shellif'amim kasheh li, ki
rak kach ani yodea'/yoda'at

תּוֹדָה, שֶׁלִּפְעָמִים קָשֶׁה לִי,
כִּי רַק כָּךְ אֲנִי יוֹדֵעַ/ת

leha'arich et hattov. Rak acharei
shennimtza'im bachoshech, efshar
leha'arich et ha'or.

לְהַעֲרִיךְ אֶת הַטּוֹב. רַק אַחֲרֵי
שֶׁנִּמְצָאִים בַּחֹשֶׁךְ, אֶפְשָׁר
לְהַעֲרִיךְ אֶת הָאוֹר.

Todah, al hachayyim hannifla'im
shennatatta li.

תּוֹדָה, עַל הַחַיִּים הַנִּפְלָאִים
שֶׁנָּתַתָּ לִי.

Todah al haddavar hachi katan
sheyyeish li, ki et hakkol attah
natatta li, velo af echad acheir.

תּוֹדָה עַל הַדָּבָר הֲכִי קָטָן
שֶׁיֵּשׁ לִי, כִּי אֶת הַכֹּל אַתָּה
נָתַתָּ לִי, וְלֹא אַף אֶחָד אַחֵר.

Todah, she'attah tamid shomea' et
hattefillot shelli, veshel am yisra'el.

תּוֹדָה, שֶׁאַתָּה תָּמִיד שׁוֹמֵעַ אֶת
הַתְּפִלּוֹת שֶׁלִּי, וְשֶׁל עַם יִשְׂרָאֵל.

Borei olam, ani mevakkesh/
mevakkeshet mimmecha selichah
mimma'amakkei libbi im hayu
pe'amim shello he'erachti et mah
shennatatta li uvimkom lomar
lecha todah rak hitlonanti. Anna al
tirchak mimmenni le'olam, ani afar
va'eifer ve'attah kol ha'olam.

בּוֹרֵא עוֹלָם, אֲנִי מְבַקֵּשׁ/ת
מִמְּךָ סְלִיחָה
מִמַּעֲמַקֵּי לִבִּי אִם הָיוּ
פְּעָמִים שֶׁלֹּא הֶעֱרַכְתִּי אֶת מָה
שֶׁנָּתַתָּ לִי וּבִמְקוֹם לוֹמַר
לְךָ תּוֹדָה רַק הִתְלוֹנַנְתִּי. אָנָּא אַל
תִּרְחַק מִמֶּנִּי לְעוֹלָם, אֲנִי עָפָר
וָאֵפֶר וְאַתָּה כָּל הָעוֹלָם.

Notes

_____

_____

_____

_____

_____

Dedicated to

The brave men and women of the Israel Defense Forces, whose unwavering courage and commitment safeguard the nation.

The hostages currently held by Hamas, for whom we pray every day. May they soon be returned to their families.

The resilient people of Israel, recognizing the strength and unity of their hearts, souls, and minds.

May these prayers bring solace and fortitude to all believers, and may they serve as a beacon of hope and faith for the entire nation.

Christine Zelm

Dedicated to

Paul and Michael Ortiz, *of blessed memory*

They loved their family above all else.

Mike, with his infectious sense of humor, brought laughter to every family gathering. His love for his family was boundless.

Paul, a shining light, naturally drew people to him with his warmth and kindness.

As the firstborn and second born, they embraced their roles as protectors of the family with unwavering dedication. Their love for their family was immense, and their memory will forever be treasured. They were and will always be loved.

Their loving parents

Thanking God for these words,

written down for us in ages past, to encourage and establish
us in His unwavering faithfulness amidst every storm.

May all who read and meditate on these prayers
be strengthened and filled with hope,
even in the darkest of seasons.

We pray for all who mourn the loss of their loved ones due to
the events of October 7th, 2023, and the ongoing war. May
they find solace in these words, penned for times such as this.

To the arrows in our quiver, our children
Santosh, Abhishek, and Divya, may the Psalms bring joy,
comfort, strength, and song to all your days!

Susan and Mathew Mathews